A Practical Guide to Transportation and Logistics

A Practical Guide

to Transportation

and Logistics

Michael B. Stroh

Second Edition

The Logistics Network
Dumont, NJ

Publisher's Cataloging-in-Publication Data
Stroh, Michael B., 1956-
       A Practical Guide to Transportation and Logistics / Michael B. Stroh.-2nd ed.
               p.   cm.
       Includes bibliographical references and index.
ISBN 0-9708115-0-0
1. Logistics.   2. Transportation.   I. Title.
                       2001

                                                          2001116238
                                                          CIP

Although the author and publisher have made every effort to ensure the accuracy and completeness of information contained in this book, we assume no responsibility for errors, inaccuracies, omissions, or any inconsistency herein. Any slights of people, places, or organizations are unintentional.

All brand names and product names mentioned in this book are trademarks or service marks of their respective companies. Any omission or misuse (of any kind) of service marks or trademarks should not be regarded as intent to infringe on the property of others. The publisher recognizes and respects all marks used by companies, manufacturers, and developers as a means to distinguish their products.

ISBN 0-9708115-0-0 (PBK)

Library of Congress Card Number: 2001116238

Books published by The Logistics Network are available at special quantity discounts for use in corporate training programs. For more information, please write to the Director of Special Sales, The Logistics Network, P.O. Box 382, Dumont, NJ 07628-2114.

To Joanie, Jimmy and Brian,
who make everything worthwhile.

Table of Contents

Table of Figures

Preface

The idea for this work came as a way for me to provide a useful tool to the distribution personnel at my company's various sites. As corporate Traffic Manager, I have the responsibility for training all of these folks and making sure that they are capable of handling most daily operational issues independently. I have conducted numerous training sessions with them, but wanted to develop something simple, yet useful, for them to refer to on an ongoing basis. Therefore, I decided to put together this little work to do just that.

While I don't mind fielding phone calls with questions from my various locations, I thought that something like this, which addresses most routine issues, may enable the remote sites to develop a feeling of independence from the corporate office. Plus, it may also serve as a means of me keeping my travel budget under control. Those trips from the east coast to the west coast can get real expensive.

What qualifies me to write such a work as this? Well, for one, I've been living this business for the past twenty-some years. I have and still do confront the same problems every day that you do. Second, I have a BS degree in transportation from St. John's University in New York and worked my way through a once great technical program offered by the now-defunct Academy of Advanced Traffic. I am a member of the Council of Logistics Management (CLM), a certified member of the American Society of Transportation and Logistics (AST&L) and SOLE – The International Society of Logistics. Finally, I have an MBA in Global Management from the University of Phoenix. This has given me a great background from an overall management standpoint. I hope that answers your question.

Well, here we go!

Introduction

This is intended for the front-line supervisor or manager fighting the daily battle to keep up with the demands our businesses place upon us. It is presented as a ***practical*** guide for doing real work. There isn't any groundbreaking new research presented here. If you are looking for state-of-the-art computer models for running a transportation function, you won't find it here. This work is a tool and nothing else. I hope it will help make your life easier.

I have been in the same boat as you for the past 20 or so years. Sometimes it isn't pretty. I've been down that road where you're putting out one fire after another, and all of a sudden, somebody comes up and drops another crisis in your lap. I'd like to think that by providing a guide such as this to you, written in an easy to read format, you'll be able to quickly find the answer you're looking for and be able to then move on to the next problem.

I have written this with the understanding that you may have absolutely no background in the field. It may be your first job or you may have recently been transferred from another functional area. As such, it is presented on a very elementary level. I'll also try to keep the use of industry jargon to a minimum. When technical terms are introduced, I will explain them completely.

Odds are, you are working for a relatively small operation with broad responsibilities. These could include shipping & receiving, the warehouse, and overall traffic administration functions. You probably do not have as much of a staff as you feel you need. I'd like to give you the benefit of my years of experience in running a day-to-day operation, which will hopefully make you more effective. Hey, if you can show your boss that you can save the company some money or speed-up the flow of your operation, you may get to be hero of the day. If nothing else, after absorbing what I have here, you can sound like an expert. Sometimes that goes a long way.

The material will be presented in a casual, almost light-hearted manner. I don't want you falling asleep in the middle of it. There is no need to read the whole work from cover to cover. Use it as a reference manual. Of course, if you want to you certainly can read it from start to finish, I won't mind. You may also notice that the discussion is very general in most cases. If you need an in-depth treatment of certain topics, there are a good number of excellent books on the market available to you. I will include a section with a recommended reading list.

Additionally, please note that I provide no coverage of two modes of transportation - rail and pipeline. This is done for a few reasons. One is that I have no direct practical experience with either of them. This is intended as a practical guide, so with no practical experience to share, I would only be spouting textbook material to you. That is not the product I want to deliver. Second, most people really have limited, if any exposure to both modes. Unless you work for an oil or gas company, or ship by the trainload, you really have no need for the discussion. If this is a shortcoming, I'm sorry. But too bad, it's my call.

One final note. This isn't such a bad field to be in. I have been in an assortment of operational and administrative positions over the last 20 years and it has provided me with a good living. You definitely could do a lot worse.

Happy reading. May the force be with you!

Overview

The Role of Transportation & Logistics in the Organization

I'd like to start off by defining what may be a new word - **logistics**. It sounds real impressive, doesn't it? Well, it is. Actually, logistics has its origin in the military. From that perspective, it refers to the movement of troops, equipment and supplies from one location to another. The people who develop management theory like to borrow military terms. Hey, competition can be a lot like combat. Anyway, these management gurus thought logistics was a great term for use in a business setting. And I really can't disagree with them. I like it too. Maybe it's the four years I spent in the U.S. Army that did it. Nonetheless, logistics became a business term. The definitive definition, as given by the Council of Logistics Management is: "…that part of the supply chain process that plans, implements, and controls the efficient, effective flow and storage of goods, services, and related information from the point of origin to the point of consumption in order to meet customers' requirements."

Business Logistics, as it is correctly called, can encompass a number of related functional areas. In its broadest sense, it can include traffic/transportation, warehousing, import/export operations, inventory control, purchasing, and customer service or sales order entry. That's a lot of ground to cover. In many companies, the logistics department will typically include the areas of traffic, warehousing and the import/export operation. Many times purchasing and inventory are included as well. Our focus will be on the areas of traffic/transportation, import/export and warehousing. This is just an arbitrary decision on my part to keep it simple and address the areas where I feel the typical logistics person would have general responsibility. If I short-shrifted one of your functional areas, oh well. Maybe I'll deal with it another time. Maybe not.

Through the balance of this work, I'm going to use the term *logistics*, rather than the longer *business logistics*, to keep it simple. I will also use logistics, transportation and traffic almost interchangeably. Is that entirely accurate? No, but that is just the convention I'll use. It's close enough.

I'll tell you right up front, in many companies, the logistics department is treated like a poor step-child. That's not a good position to be in. Many other functional areas look at what we do as just an expense for the company - a necessary evil. I've heard the following comment from a company controller I used to work with, "What's the big deal? You just pick-up the phone, call the truck in, throw the boxes on the back and your done. How hard is that?" Does this sound familiar to anyone? Comments like that can really brighten your spirits. Especially if you have just been beat up by almost everybody in the company all day long.

Now for the good news. This opinion is starting to change, and fast. Many senior executives are now realizing the value provided by the logistics department. We are now being seen as an area that can help reduce overall costs for the company and add value to the product for the customer. There are now many companies with senior level executives with logistics titles. It's been a long, hard battle but the tide is starting to turn.

In an organization, the lead logistics person can go by a number of different titles. Some of the more common ones I've seen are logistics manager, traffic manager, transportation manager, supply-chain manager, purchasing manager or distribution manager. "A rose by any other name..." Take your pick.

Chapter 1

Domestic Transportation

Domestic transportation is that which takes place within the confines of the fifty states. Depending upon the carrier, Puerto Rico can, in some sense, be considered a domestic move as well. This is the simplest aspect of your area of responsibility. This is what the oversimplifying executive thinks of when logistics comes to mind. And even this can be quite a hassle under the proper, or improper, conditions as the case may be.

In talking about simple things, I'd like to introduce something called Pareto's Law. For those of you familiar with the concept, just indulge me for a minute.

Pareto's law is quite simple and, from my experience, quite accurate. It is also known as the 80-20 Rule. As it applies to your workload, what it states is that 20% of your assignments account for 80% of your time and/or resources. In other words, you spend 80% of your day dealing with a small percentage of "problem children". Does that hit home for anyone? I know it does for me.

So yeah, in many cases, shipping a piece of freight is as simple as just calling in the carrier and putting the box or skid on the truck. It's that 20% that kills you day in and day out. So when you've just finished cleaning up after the mess created by one of the 20% and someone tells you how easy you've got it, you want to strangle the guy (woman).

Pareto applies to many different areas that the logistics manager can encounter. One quite common scenario is concerning inventory. Typically, 20% of the inventory in a warehouse comprises 80% of the activity. If you can manage this 20% well, you're mostly home free. We'll cover this in more detail when we get to the warehousing section.

Overview of the Domestic Transportation Scene

Domestic transportation within the U.S. used to be a highly regulated industry. The rail industry was first regulated way back in 1887 by the first Act to Regulate Commerce. This act created the once imposing Interstate Commerce Commission (ICC). The Act and the Commission were created to curb abuses within the rail industry. Primary among these were discrimination favoring one shipper over another; rebates given by a carrier to a shipper or prospective shipper to obtain or maintain business; special rates favoring certain shippers; rates were not published; and the rate system was confusing and complex.

The motor carrier industry was not regulated until 1935. In that year the Motor Carrier Act, 1935 was passed. Its purpose was to bring stabilization to an industry that was viewed as chaotic at the time. The act defined three different classes of carriers: common carriers, contract carriers and private carriers. Briefly, a common carrier is one who holds his services out to the general public. A contract carrier is one who offers their services to one or a limited number of persons under the terms of a contract. Finally, a private carrier is a situation where a company would operate its own fleet of vehicles.

The domestic air carrier industry was first regulated in the 1920s and 1930s. The first comprehensive legislation passed was the Civil Aeronautics Act of 1938. This created the Civil Aeronautics Board as the governing authority for domestic air transportation. The Federal Aviation Act supplemented this law in 1958.

In the late 1970s, the transportation industry and the federal government realized that the current regulatory environment was an impediment to competition and a movement began to deregulate the industry.

The air cargo industry was the first to deregulate itself back in 1977. Then in 1980, the floodgates opened and the rail industry was deregulated with the passing of the Staggers Rail Act of 1980 and the motor carriers were deregulated by the Motor Carrier Act of 1980. This trend continued through the 1980s and 1990s.

In 1985, the governing body for the airline industry, the Civil Aeronautics Board, was sunsetted (dissolved). This was followed-up by the Federal Aviation Act of 1994 which eliminated all interstate economic regulation of the industry by the federal government.

The motor carrier industry was the subject of a number of pieces of legislation in the early- to mid- part of the 1990s. The Negotiated Rates Act of 1993 was implemented with the purpose of protecting shippers from a flood of overcharge claims from bankrupt carriers. The overcharge claims resulted from the then illegal practice of implementing discounts without filing them with the Interstate Commerce Commission (ICC). Then, in 1994, Congress passed the Trucking Industry Regulatory Reform Act. The main provision of this law was to repeal the *filed rate doctrine*. With the implementation of this law, a motor carrier was no longer required to file its rates and rules with the ICC.

Finally, in 1995, the ICC Termination Act was passed eliminating the Interstate Commerce Commission. The remaining powers of this once formidable agency were transferred to the Surface Transportation Board (Surf Board), which is an independent board within the Department of Transportation (DOT). A further consequence of this Act was the elimination of the distinction between common and contract carriers.

Ground Transportation

Truckload (TL)

As the name implies, a truckload carrier is one that moves single shipments, which fill-out the visible capacity of a trailer. They pick-up the freight at one particular shipper and deliver that freight to one particular consignee (customer or receiving location). With that being said, depending upon the nature of the freight - namely its size and density, a full truckload may not fill the visible capacity of a trailer. Typically, if a shipment weighs in excess of 36,000 pounds (#), then it qualifies as a truckload, whether or not the trailer is full.

There are a number of advantages to moving freight in truckload quantities. The two primary benefits are cost and time. A truckload volume will almost always result in a lower cost per pound than a less-than-truckload volume. A general rule in freight pricing is that the higher the weight, the lower the rate (cost) per pound. This is a result of carrier efficiencies derived from moving larger shipments. Carriers have a number of standard costs per shipment regardless of its size. They still have to pick-up the freight; they have to move it from place to place; they have to deliver it; they have to generate a freight bill; and they have to collect the payment. This is characteristic of every shipment. The fewer pick-ups, deliveries and invoices they must generate per truck, the more efficient they are. Consequently, you the shipper derive some of the benefit of this efficiency.

You also gain the benefit of time by shipping in truckload volumes. If a truck can move directly from origin to destination, with no intermediate deliveries, you can get to your destination much quicker. On a cross-country move, a less-than-truckload (LTL) shipment may make three or four stops for reloading and re-consolidation before it reaches its ultimate destination. On the other hand, a TL move will generally make no stops in between. A coast-to-coast truckload (TL) move, with a team of two drivers, can be delivered in two to three days. A typical LTL move of the same distance ordinarily takes five to six working days. This is a tremendous difference.

One other approach to truckload traffic is to tender two or more large LTL shipments to the carrier, achieve the benefit of the truckload rate, and pay an additional charge for stop-offs. This only works if the shipments are headed in the same general direction. If your origin is Los Angeles and you have destination points of Houston, Detroit and Miami, it won't work well.

There are a multitude of truckload carriers on the market just dying to grab a piece of your business. Some of the larger, better known TL carriers are:

- Schneider National
- J.B. Hunt
- Ryder Dedicated Logistics
- Werner Enterprises

Less-Than-Truckload (LTL)

This is the most typical type of truck shipping you will encounter in your daily routine. Most of the "household name" trucking companies are less-than-truckload (LTL) carriers. The LTL carrier picks-up an assortment of small shipments from a number of different shippers over the course of a day's pick-up run. At the end of the day, the hopefully full truck returns to the local terminal, the freight is sorted, based upon general destination, and reloaded on other trucks headed for that general direction. Along the way, the freight may make two or three additional stops at various "break-bulk" points. These are terminals where the freight will be unloaded again, re-sorted and reloaded as the freight draws closer to its ultimate destination. Finally, the freight reaches its destination terminal where it is unloaded again, re-sorted and loaded on delivery trucks for delivery to the ultimate consignee (customer). As mentioned in our discussion of TL carriers, LTL moves can be time consuming thanks to the numerous stops and sorts the freight must go through. Each stop and re-sort also increases the likelihood of the freight getting lost or damaged.

Again, a typical coast-to-coast move will typically take five to six working days. Weekends do not count in the transit time calculation. The pick-up day doesn't count either. For example, if you ship something on a Wednesday in New York City, with an ultimate destination of Los Angeles, and the carrier has a transit time of six days, you would calculate the estimated time of delivery to Thursday of the following week. You eliminate the pick-up day of Wednesday, plus Saturday and Sunday, thereby arriving on Thursday of the next week.

Some carriers eliminate or minimize the extra handling of the typical break-bulk operation. They are commonly referred to as load-to-ride carriers. By eliminating as many as three freight handlings, these carriers offer shortened transit times and fewer loss and damage issues. True load-to-ride carriers do a final sort at the origin terminal and route the freight for final delivery directly onto the road trailer. Without break-bulk consolidation, delivery cost is higher. For this reason, load-to-ride carriers cannot economically justify small LTL shipments. Typically, these carriers can provide improved efficiency on shipments of 1,500# or greater. One of the better-known carriers in this market is Jevic Transportation.

LTL carriers can be broken-up into two major categories: long-haul and short-haul. Long-haul carriers will generally serve destinations that are over 300 miles from the origin terminal. Short-haul carriers, on the other hand, serve those points within a 300 mile radius of the origin terminal. Short-haul carriers can also be referred to as regional carriers.

There is another category of carrier known as a super regional. They cover more of a geographic scope than the traditional short-haul carrier, yet they do not cover as much as the typical long-haul carrier.

An important point to consider when choosing a carrier: not all carriers directly serve all points within the geographic region they cover. In such a case, the common practice is for the originating carrier to turn the freight over to a local carrier for delivery. This practice is called **interlining**. In such a case the two carriers divide the revenue between them on a percentage basis, dependent upon how much each carrier performed in providing the overall service. Interline shipments will generally add at least one extra day to the transit time of the move. It takes time to transfer the freight between the two carriers. Also, your discount with the originating carrier will generally not apply so you will pay the full tariff rate for the move, which can be quite expensive. Check the service guide provided by your carrier before turning the freight over to him. Because if it is an interline point you are shipping to, you may be in for a not so pleasant surprise.

Some of the more well-known LTL carriers are:

- Yellow Freight
- Roadway Express
- Consolidated Freightways
- ABF Freight System
- Overnite Transportation
- American Freightways
- The USF group of regional carriers
- The Conway group of regional carriers

Brokers

A transportation broker is a company that generally owns no trucks of their own. They solicit shipments from various shippers and mate them up with owner-operators looking for freight. An owner-operator is an individual who owns his own truck. Rather obvious, right. These folks are always looking for freight to keep themselves in business and they, and the brokers, work together to provide a generally low-cost means of moving larger LTL and truckload shipments.

The broker bills the shipper for the freight, then pays the owner-operator a percentage of the revenue for the transportation service provided. The broker is paid for his efforts in matching-up the load with a truck, billing for the freight charges and collecting the revenue. The owner-operator is paid for the actual movement of the freight. It is a beneficial relationship for both parties. It is also a good, economical means of moving freight for the shipper.

One word of caution though: not all brokers are created equal. Before you choose a broker, ensure you know whom you are dealing with. While most brokers are reputable operations using good owner-operators, some are fly-by-night shops scouring the local truck stops for trucks. Ask for a reference list of customers and check those references. Also, ask for a current certificate of insurance, sent to you directly by the insurance company, to verify that they have cargo insurance should something happen to the freight in-transit. You wouldn't want to have the freight get damaged, only to find out later that the broker has no insurance to cover it. Finally, if the broker does not pay the owner-operator for the move, they could conceivably come after the shipper for payment. I cannot stress enough; *know the company with whom you are doing business*. It can save you a world of grief down the road.

Shipping Documents

There are three primary documents used in a domestic truck shipment. These are the bill of lading (B/L), the carrier freight bill and the delivery receipt (D/R). They are all quite important and we will now discuss them individually.

Bill of Lading (B/L)

The Interstate Commerce Commission in 1919 prescribed the standard format for the bill of lading. There are two different types of bills of lading - the straight bill of lading and the order bill of lading. The straight bill of lading is the most common. The order bill of lading is used as a means for the shipper to obtain payment for the goods from the customer.

Let me digress for a moment. The terms "shipper" and "consignor" are interchangeable in transportation lingo. This is the company, or person, who gives the freight to the carrier for shipment. The recipient of the freight, or customer, is typically referred to as the "consignee." That is the person to whom the freight is "consigned." These are frequently used transportation terms and you need to know what they mean.

Okay, back to the original discussion. An order bill of lading is equal in value to the value of the goods shipped. It is what is known as a negotiable document. When an order bill of lading is used, the consignee may not take possession of the goods shipped until they pay for them. The consignor presents the original order bill of lading, along with a draft for collection of the value of the goods, to his bank. The shipper's bank then presents these documents to the customer's bank for collection. When the consignee pays his bank the value of the goods shipped, his bank will then surrender the original order bill of lading to the consignee. The consignee's bank then forwards the proceeds from the collection to the shipper's bank. The shipper's bank then pays the shipper. Then, when the freight is offered for delivery, the consignee can turn over the order bill of lading to the carrier and he, in turn, will deliver the freight.

Is that clear? Yeah, sure, about as clear as mud you say! Just wait until we talk about letters of credit in the international sections of this work. Don't worry. In the 20 years I've been in logistics, I have never encountered an order bill of lading. Nonetheless, you should know they exist and what they are, just in case.

The straight bill of lading is what you will ordinarily see and use in virtually all shipping transactions. The straight bill of lading comes in two flavors: regular and the short form. The only difference between the two is that the short form does not contain the contract terms and conditions on the reverse side. These terms and conditions are referenced and implied though.

The bill of lading serves three primary purposes. These are:

- A receipt from the carrier to the shipper for the goods received for transportation.
- A contract of carriage.
- A presumption of title to the goods.

The bill of lading should contain the following information:

- Shipper's name and address.
- Consignee's name and address.
- A description of the goods offered for transport.
- The gross weight of the shipment.
- An indication of who pays the freight charges - the shipper, the consignee, or a third-party.

Other information can be provided, but at minimum, the above must be included. There are examples of the various types of bills of lading in figures 1,2 & 3, illustrating how they look.

An important note! If you are shipping on a collect basis, in other words, your customer is paying the freight charges, ensure that you sign your name in section seven (7) of the bill of lading. This is typically located in a block on the right side of the bill of lading. By signing in this block, you release your company from any liability for the freight charges should your customer fail to pay the carrier. *Make sure you sign this!*

Figure 1

SUPPLEMENT 1 TO NMF 100-V

RULES

(Cancels "Uniform Order Bill of Lading" appearing on page 258 of tariff.)
(To be Printed on Yellow Paper)

UNIFORM ORDER BILL OF LADING
Original—Domestic

Shipper's No. _____

Agent's No. _____

_____ Carrier_____ (SCAC)

☼RECEIVED, subject to the classifications and tariffs in effect on the date of the issue of this Bill of Lading.

From _____ Date _____ 19_____

At _____ Street _____ City _____ County _____ State ___ Zip ___

the property described below, in apparent good order, except as noted (contents and condition of contents of packages unknown) marked, consigned, and destined as shown below, which said company (the word company being understood throughout this contract as meaning any person or corporation in possession of the property under the contract) agrees to carry to its usual place of delivery at said destination, if on its own railroad, water line, highway route or routes, or within the territory of its highway operations, otherwise to deliver to another carrier on the route to said destination. It is mutually agreed, as to each carrier of all or any of said property over all or any portion of said route to destination, and as to each party at any time interested in all or any of said property, that every service to be performed hereunder shall be subject to all the conditions not prohibited by law, whether printed or written, herein contained, including the conditions on the back hereof, which are hereby agreed to by the shipper and accepted for himself and his assigns.

The surrender of this Original ORDER Bill of Lading properly indorsed shall be required before the delivery of the property. Inspection of property conveyed by this bill of lading will not be permitted unless provided by law or unless permission is indorsed on this original bill of lading or given in writing by the shipper.

Consigned to Order of _____ ____

Destination _____ Street _____ City _____ County _____ State ___ Zip ___

Notify _____

At _____ Street _____ City _____ County _____ State ___ Zip ___

Routing _____

Delivering Carrier _____ Vehicle or Car Initial _____ No. _____

No. Pack-ages	⊙ HM	Description of Articles (Subject to Correction), Kind of Package, Special Marks and Exceptions (See NMFC Item (Rule) 360)	*Weight (Subject to Correction)	Class or Rate (For Informational Purposes Only)	Subject to Section 7 of conditions, if the shipment is to be delivered to the consignee without recourse on the consignor, the consignor shall sign the following statement:
					The carrier shall not make delivery of this shipment without payment of freight and all other lawful charges.
					(Signature of consignor)
					If charges are to be prepaid write or stamp here "To be Prepaid."
					Received $ _____
					to apply in prepayment of the charges on the property described hereon.
					Agent or Cashier
					Per _____
					(The signature here acknowledges only the amount prepaid)

*If the shipment moves between two ports by a carrier by water, the law requires that the bill of lading shall state whether it is "carrier's or shipper's weight."

NOTE—(1) Where the rate is dependent on value, shippers are required to state specifically in writing the agreed or declared value of the property, as follows:

"The agreed or declared value of the property is hereby specifically stated by the shipper to be not exceeding _____ per _____."

(2) Where the applicable tariff provisions specify a limitation of the carrier's liability absent a release or a value declaration by the shipper and the shipper does not release the carrier's liability or declare a value, the carrier's liability shall be limited to the extent provided by such provisions. See NMFC Item 172.

Charges advanced:

$ _____

_____ Shipper _____ Agent

Per _____ Per _____

Permanent address of Shipper: Street _____ City _____ State _____ Zip _____

⊙ Mark with "X" to designate Hazardous Materials as defined in the Department of Transportation Regulations governing the transportation of hazardous materials. The use of this column is an optional method for identifying hazardous materials on bills of lading per Section 172.201(a)(1)(iii) of Title 49, Code of Federal Regulations. Also, when shipping hazardous materials, the shipper's certification statement prescribed in Section 172.204(a) of the Federal Regulations must be indicated on the bill of lading, unless a specific exception from this requirement is provided in the Regulations for a particular material.

Cancellation of the phrase "lawfully filed" previously shown in connection with these provisions has been suspended in I. & S. Docket M-30440 to and including November 28, 1995. Apply provisions otherwise provided.

16   For explanation of abbreviations and reference marks, see last page(s) of this supplement.   ©ATA 1995

Figure 2   SUPPLEMENT 1 TO NMF 100-V

RULES

(Cancels "Uniform Straight Bill of Lading" appearing on page 255 of tariff.)

(To be Printed on White Paper)

UNIFORM STRAIGHT BILL OF LADING

ORIGINAL—NOT NEGOTIABLE—Domestic

Shipper's No._____

Agent's No._____

Carrier _____ (SCAC)

☼RECEIVED, subject to the classifications and tariffs in effect on the date of the issue of this Bill of Lading.

From _____   Date _____ 19 _____

Street _____ City _____ County _____ State _____ Zip _____

the property described below, in apparent good order, except as noted (contents and condition of contents of packages unknown) marked, consigned, and destined as shown below, which said company (the word company being understood throughout this contract as meaning any person or corporation in possession of the property under the contract) agrees to carry to its usual place of delivery at said destination, if on its own railroad, water line, highway route or routes, or within the territory of its highway operations, otherwise to deliver to another carrier on the route to said destination. It is mutually agreed, as to each carrier of all or any of said property over all or any portion of said route to destination, and as to each party at any time interested in all or any of said property, that every service to be performed hereunder shall be subject to all the conditions not prohibited by law, whether printed or written, herein contained, including the conditions on the back hereof, which are hereby agreed to by the shipper and accepted for himself and his assigns.

Consigned to _____

On Collect on Delivery Shipments, the letters "COD" must appear before consignee's name.

Street _____

City _____ County _____ State _____ Zip _____

Routing _____

Delivering Carrier _____ Vehicle or Car Initial _____ No. _____

**Collect on Delivery $ _____ and remit to:

_____ Street _____ City _____ State

C.O.D. charge	Shipper	☐
to be paid by	Consignee	☐

No. Pack-ages	✪ HM	Description of Articles (Subject to Correction), Kind of Package, Special Marks, and Exceptions (See NMFC Item (Rule) 360)	*Weight (Subject to Correction)	Class or Rate (For Informational Purposes Only)

Subject to Section 7 of conditions, if the shipment is to be delivered to the consignee without recourse on the consignor, the consignor shall sign the following statement:

The carrier shall not make delivery of this shipment without payment of freight and all other lawful charges.

_____
(Signature of consignor)

If charges are to be prepaid write or stamp here "To be Prepaid."

Received $ _____ to apply to prepayment of the charges on the property described hereon.

Agent or Cashier

Per _____
(The signature here acknowledges only the amount prepaid)

*If the shipment moves between two ports by a carrier by water, the law requires that the bill of lading shall state whether it is "carrier's or shipper's weight."

NOTE—(1) Where the rate is dependent on value, shippers are required to state specifically in writing the agreed or declared value of the property, as follows:

"The agreed or declared value of the property is hereby specifically stated by the shipper to be not exceeding _____ per _____."

(2) Where the applicable tariff provisions specify a limitation of the carrier's liability absent a release or a value declaration by the shipper and the shipper does not release the carrier's liability or declare a value, the carrier's liability shall be limited to the extent provided by such provisions. See NMFC Item 172.

Charges advanced:

$ _____

_____ Shipper _____ Agent

Per _____ Per _____

Permanent address of Shipper: Street _____ City _____ State _____

**Recommended C.O.D. Section to be Printed in Red.

✪ Mark with "X" to designate Hazardous Materials as defined in the Department of Transportation Regulations governing the transportation of hazardous materials. The use of this column is an optional method for identifying hazardous materials on bills of lading per Section 172.201(a)(1)(iii) of Title 49, Code of Federal Regulations. Also, when shipping hazardous materials, the shipper's certification statement prescribed in Section 172.204(a) of the Federal Regulations must be indicated on the bill of lading, unless a specific exception from this requirement is provided in the Regulations for a particular material.

Cancellation of the phrase "lawfully filed" previously shown in connection with these provisions has been suspended in I. & S. Docket M-30-40 to and including November 28, 1995. Apply provisions otherwise provided.

For explanation of abbreviations and reference marks, see last page(s) of this supplement. ©ATA 1995   13

Figure 3

RULES

(Cancels "Straight Bill of Lading - Short Form" appearing on page 261 of tariff.)

STRAIGHT BILL OF LADING — SHORT FORM

ORIGINAL – NOT NEGOTIABLE
(To be printed on white paper)

Shipper's No. _____

(Name of Carrier) _____ (SCAC) _____ Carrier's No. _____

✿ RECEIVED, subject to the classifications and tariffs in effect on the date of the issue of this Bill of Lading.

At _____ 19 _____

From _____

the property described below, in apparent good order, except as noted (contents and condition of contents of packages unknown) marked, consigned, and destined as shown below, which said carrier (the word carrier being understood throughout this contract as meaning any person or corporation in possession of the property under the contract) agrees to carry to its usual place of delivery at said destination, if on its route, otherwise to deliver to another carrier on the route to said destination. It is mutually agreed, as to each carrier of all or any of said property over all or any portion of said route to destination, and as to each party at any time interested in all or any of said property, that every service to be performed hereunder shall be subject to all the terms and conditions of the Uniform Domestic Straight Bill of Lading set forth (1) in Uniform Freight Classification in effect on the date hereof, if this is a rail or rail-water shipment, or (2) in the applicable motor carrier classification or tariff if this is a motor carrier shipment.

Shipper hereby certifies that he is familiar with all the terms and conditions of the said bill of lading, including those on the back thereof, set forth in the classification or tariff which governs the transportation of this shipment, and the said terms and conditions are hereby agreed to by the shipper and accepted for himself and his assigns.

Consigned to _____

On Collect on Delivery shipments, the letters "COD" must appear before consignee's name.

(Mail or street address of consignee — For purposes of notification only)

Destination _____ State _____ County _____

Zip

Delivery Address* _____ (*To be filled in only when shipper desires and governing tariffs provide for delivery thereof) _____

Route _____

Delivering Carrier _____ Car or Vehicle Initials _____ No. _____

No. Packages	✿ HM	Description of Articles (Subject to Correction), Kind of Package, Special Marks and Exceptions (See NMFC Item (Rule) 360)	*Weight (Subject to Correction)	Class or Rate (For Informational Purposes Only)	Subject to Section 7 of conditions, if this shipment is to be delivered to the consignee without recourse on the consignor, the consignor shall sign the following statement:
					The carrier shall not make delivery of this shipment without payment of freight and all other lawful charges.
					_____ (Signature of consignor)
					If charges are to be prepaid, write or stamp here "To be Prepaid."
					Received $ _____ to apply to prepayment of the charges on the property described hereon.
					Agent or Cashier
					Per _____ (The signature here acknowledges only the amount prepaid)
					Charges advanced $

*If the shipment moves between two ports by a carrier by water, the law requires that the bill of lading shall state whether it is "carrier's or shipper's weight."

NOTE — (1) Where the rate is dependent on value, shippers are required to state specifically in writing the agreed or declared value of the property, as follows:

"The agreed or declared value of the property is hereby specifically stated by the shipper to be not exceeding _____ per _____."

(2) Where the applicable tariff provisions specify a limitation of the carrier's liability absent a release or a value declaration by the shipper and the shipper does not release the carrier's liability or declare a value, the carrier's liability shall be limited to the extent provided by such provisions. See NMFC Item 172.

_____ Shipper _____ Agent

Per _____ Per _____

Permanent post office address of shipper _____

❍ Mark with "X" to designate Hazardous Materials as defined in the Department of Transportation Regulations governing the transportation of hazardous materials. The use of this column is an optional method for identifying hazardous materials on bills of lading per Section 172.201(a)(1)(iii) of Title 49, Code of Federal Regulations. Also, when shipping hazardous materials, the shipper's certification statement prescribed in Section 172.204(a) of the Federal Regulations must be indicated on the bill of lading, unless a specific exception from this requirement is provided in the Regulations for a particular material.

Cancellation of the phrase lawfully filed previously shown in connection with these provisions has been suspended in I.C.A. & T Docket M-30100 effective November 20, 1995. Apply provisions otherwise provided.

For explanation of abbreviations and reference marks, see last page(s) of this supplement. ©ATA 1995   19

Carrier Freight Bill

The carrier freight bill is an invoice presented by the carrier to either the shipper, the consignee or a referenced third-party as a demand for payment for services rendered. Like the bill of lading, it is a pretty standard document. It will show, at minimum, the name of the carrier, the carrier's reference number (pro number), the shipper's name and address, consignee's name and address, a description of the goods, the rate, the freight terms and the charges due. Check these documents very carefully. Carriers are not perfect and they have been known to make mistakes in preparing their invoices. As the recipient of this freight bill, it is your obligation to ensure that you were billed properly for your shipment. An example of a typical carrier freight bill is presented in figure 4.

Delivery Receipt (D/R)

The delivery receipt is a document, issued by the carrier, which the consignee signs as proof of receipt. It is also known as a proof of delivery (POD). The D/R contains essentially the same information as the freight bill and the bill of lading. The consignee signs and dates the delivery receipt upon receipt of the goods delivered. The carrier retains a copy and the consignee retains a copy. An example is presented in figure 5.

If the freight is damaged at the time of delivery, be sure that you note on the delivery receipt that the goods are damaged. Describe briefly the nature and extent of the damage. If you cannot fully ascertain the extent of the damage, make a statement to the effect of, "10 boxes crushed, contents subject to further inspection." If there is visible damage upon receipt and you do not record it on the delivery receipt, you are basically dead in the water if you attempt to file a damage claim at a later date. **Be forewarned!**

Rate Development & Negotiation

This is the area where you, as the lead logistics person for your company, can either be a real hero or, if you don't handle it properly, a goat. Great time and care should be taken to ensure that your company pays no more than they need to for the transportation services they use. An extremely important point to always keep in mind is that you need to strike the right balance between price and service. The old adage that "you get what you pay for" applies quite well when it comes to purchasing transportation services. Do not sell your operation short by picking the lowest price on the block, only to find out later, after you've committed your freight to the carrier, that they can't get the job done. Always deal with reputable carriers, with a known good reputation that you can verify. There are plenty of marginal carriers out there that can make you look quite foolish at best, or seriously affect your company's relationship with their customers at worst. *Be wary!*

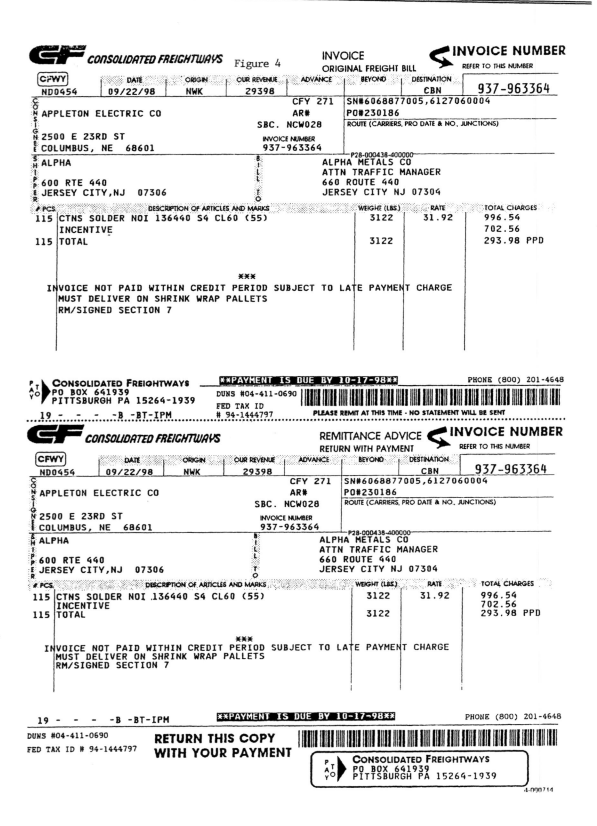

Figure 4

Figure 5

CF CONSOLIDATED FREIGHTWAYS CFWY **CONSIGNEE COPY** **INVOICE NUMBER** REFER TO THIS NUMBER

EQUIP. NUMBER	DATE	ORIGIN	CF REVENUE	ADVANCE	BEYOND	DESTINATION	
17-4728	6/08/98	NCG			[illegible]	JHK	[illegible]

CONSIGNEE
ALPHA METALS INC
JC STOCK RM
600 RT 440
JERSEY CITY,NJ 07304

CEY
AR#
S.C.

SHIPPER'S NUMBER [illegible]95 01
PO# NICOLE RICHARDSON

INVOICE NUMBER
810-976316

ROUTE (CARRIERS, PRO DATE & NO., JUNCTIONS)

SHIPPER
ALPHA METALS INC

200 TECHNOLOGY DRIVE
ALPHARETTA, GA 30202

BILL TO

# PCS.	HM	DESCRIPTION OF ARTICLES AND MARKS	WEIGHT (LBS)	RATE	TOTAL CHARGES
14		PCS CHEMICALS 60000 CL 70	700		
14		TOTAL	700		PPD
		1 SKID SAID TO CONTAIN 14			
		C OF A WITH SHIPMENTS			
		DB			
		100% SATIS[illegible] GOAL! CALL US FIRST AT (9[illegible]) 3[illegible]			

RECEIVED JUN 11 1998 By

SHRINK WRAP INTACT? ☐ YES ☐ NO ☐ INSIDE DEL ☐ CONSTRUCTION SITE ☐ REDEL ☐ SORT # PCS ____ ☐ LIFT GATE DETENTION TIME: START ____ END ____
OTHER ____

DUNS # 04-411-0990
LEAVE THIS COPY WITH CONSIGNEE

CONSOLIDATED FREIGHTWAYS CORP. OF DEL. DBA
CONSOLIDATED FREIGHTWAYS
P.O. Box 4488
Portland, Oregon 97208-4488

8

The History of Rate Making

My first technical introduction to this industry came through attending a wonderful program at a now demised school called the Academy of Advanced Traffic. I attended in the very early 1980s, just as deregulation of the industry was beginning and before the widespread use of the personal computer in business. Starting out at that point in time allowed me to get a first-hand feel for how the transportation rating process functioned for the preceding 80 years or so. Let me tell you, it was a laborious and time-consuming undertaking. For someone to audit the accuracy of a carrier freight bill required a thorough understanding of the intricacies of carrier rates and a room full of paper-bound *tariffs* (rate schedules). A good pair of reading glasses was helpful too!

Rates were developed by entities known as **rate bureaus**. Each bureau covered a specific geographic scope. In figure 6, you can see the areas covered by the major rail and motor freight bureaus of the time. Most, if not all, carriers were participating members of these bureaus. Consequently, all carriers operated off of the same rates. There was no difference in price, there were no discounts off of these bureau rates, and the various carriers competed on the basis of service alone.

Deregulation opened the industry to price competition and eventually enabled the individual carriers to publish their own tariffs, with varying rates, and offer discounts off of these rates. The proliferation of the personal computer allowed for a simplified and rapid means of determining carrier rates.

Today, each carrier develops their own rate structure for the geographic area they serve and they make these rates available for free to all of their customers on computer diskette to make the rating process easy for everyone. While the carriers, in developing their rate structures, still use the same basic process, it is far simpler now for the shipper to determine what the rate is for a particular shipment.

Finally, every carrier *discounts* their standard rates to any customer who wishes to do business with them. Only under the most extreme conditions should you ever have to pay the full tariff rate for a shipment. We will talk about these cases later.

The Theory of Rate Making

The most common method of constructing and determining freight rates for LTL transportation is through the *class rate system*. "Freight classification is the process of dividing articles shipped into a limited number of classes or groups, in order to simplify" the rate making process. (Ovens, vol. 1, p.75) Simply stated, class ratings assign freight of similar transportation characteristics similar ratings. By grouping different types of commodities together, the need to develop a specific rate for the multitude of goods that ship is eliminated. The governing publication for the rating of goods via rail is the

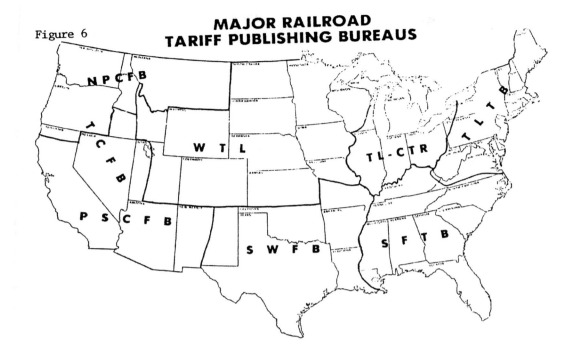

**MAJOR RAILROAD
TARIFF PUBLISHING BUREAUS**

Figure 6

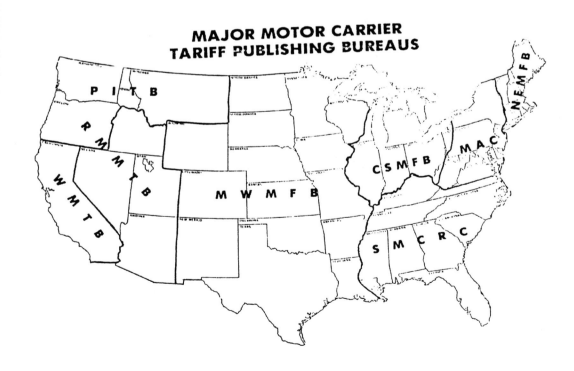

**MAJOR MOTOR CARRIER
TARIFF PUBLISHING BUREAUS**

Uniform Freight Classification (UFC). For the motor carrier industry, the governing publication is the National Motor Freight Classification (NMFC).

There are a number of principal factors used to determine the classification of freight. These are:

- Cost of service to the carrier.
- Value of service to the shipper.
- Cost of production.
- Competition.
- Value of Article.
- How shipped (TL, LTL).
- Volume of traffic and periods of movement.
- Methods of packing and protecting the article.
- Risk.
- Special facilities or extra services required.
- Dimensions (bulk) and weight. (Ovens, vol. 1, p. 82)

Class ratings range from a low of class 50 to a high of class 500. The lower the class rating, the lower the cost to ship the product. Generally, low-value freight that is easy to handle and unlikely to become damaged will receive the lowest class ratings. Conversely, high-value freight that is bulky and easily damaged will receive higher class ratings.

When a carrier constructs their rates, they use class 100, as the base class from which all other rates are determined. Class 100 is what a carrier would consider average freight with regard to all of the above listed factors. In the old days, class 50 rates were ½ of class 100 rates. Class 200 rates were twice that of class 100 rates. Over the last several years, carriers have developed more sophisticated algorithms for determining rates. But, the old method does give you some idea of the relationship between the different class ratings.

A sample class rate schedule is displayed in figure 7. This schedule shows, in a tabular format, the various classes and their associated rate per 100# depending upon the weight of the shipment. These rates reflect a shipment from Jersey City, NJ to Foster City, CA (note the two zip codes). There are columns for less than 500#, 500# to 999#, 1,000# to 1,999#, 2,000# to 4,999#, 5,000# to 9,999#, etc. The rates are expressed in dollars and cents per **hundredweight (cwt)**. In transportation parlance, this is the way you refer to increments of 100 pounds. The numbers do not indicate decimal points. So for example, the rate for a class 50 shipment at less than 500# is $64.41/100 pounds.

As well, a sample page from the National Motor Freight Classification (NMFC) is presented in figure 8.

Figure 7   CF - Miles aheaD
ORIGIN: 07304   BASE RATE %: 100.00

DEST ZIP	CLS	L1CMC	1CMC	MC	L5C	5C	1M	2M	5M	10M	20M	30M
94404	50.0	14700	18692		6441	5182	4331	3750	3267	2754	2433	2113
	55.0				6904	5553	4641	4019	3503	2953	2609	2266
	60.0				7330	5893	4926	4265	3720	3136	2771	2406
	65.0				7792	6263	5236	4533	3956	3335	2946	2559
	70.0				8239	6620	5536	4793	4184	3527	3116	2706
	77.5				8874	7128	5961	5161	4508	3800	3357	2916
	85.0				9643	7744	6476	5607	4900	4131	3650	3170
	92.5				10375	8329	6967	6032	5274	4446	3928	3411
	100.0				11092	8902	7447	6447	5639	4754	4200	3648
	110.0				12190	9781	8183	7084	6199	5227	4617	4010
	125.0				13826	11090	9279	8033	7034	5930	5239	4550
	150.0				16532	13255	11092	9603	8414	7094	6267	5443
	175.0				19209	15396	12886	11155	9779	8245	7284	6326
	200.0				21884	17536	14678	12707	11144	9396	8301	7209
	250.0				27236	21817	18264	15810	13874	11697	10334	8975
	300.0				32588	26099	21850	18915	16603	13999	12367	10741
	350.0				37939	30380	25435	22018	19333	16301	14401	12507
	400.0				43291	34661	29021	25122	22063	18602	16434	14273
	500.0				53994	43223	36193	31330	27522	23206	20501	17805

Figure 8

NATIONAL MOTOR FREIGHT CLASSIFICATION 100-V

Item	ARTICLES	CLASS
	METALS GROUP: subject to item 135300	
135720	Electrotype Base Metal, in barrels or boxes; loose when shipments weigh 36,000 pounds or more	55
135760	Gold Articles or Ware, or articles with gold parts or ornaments	Not Taken
135780	Gold Plated Ware, not on silver, NOI, in boxes	200
135782	Ferro-cobalt-nickel alloys, viz: Articles, NOI, Sheet, Strip or Tubing, in boxes; or Wire, in packages	100
135800	Ingots, beryllium-aluminum, in boxes:	
Sub 1	Beryllium content exceeding 2 percent	100
Sub 2	Beryllium content not exceeding 2 percent	85
135850	Lead Base Alloys, NOI, tin content not exceeding 10 percent:	
Sub 1	Bars, pigs or slabs	55
Sub 2	Other than bars, pigs or slabs, in packages	60
135870	OLithium Metal, in packages	100
135890	Manganese-copper, in barrels; loose or in packages when shipments weigh 36,000 pounds or more	70
135910	Manganese Metal, in barrels, boxes or in polyethylene bags enclosed in paper-lined cloth bags; loose or in bags when shipments weigh 36,000 pounds or more	60
135930	Manganese-silicon, in barrels; loose or in packages when shipments weigh 36,000 pounds or more	70
135950	Metal, thermostat:	
Sub 1	Articles, NOI, in boxes	100
Sub 2	Sheet or strip, in boxes	85
135990	Nickel Magnesium Alloy or Nickel Magnesium Silicon Alloy, viz.: Ingots, Lumps or Granules, in packages	65
136020	OPotassium (Potash), metallic, in barrels or boxes	100
136030	Powder, ferro-nickel, in steel drums	60
136040	Quicksilver (Metallic Mercury), in glass in barrels or boxes, in iron flasks, or in Package 802. See item 60000 for class dependent upon agreed or released value	200
136060	Residue, consisting of copper, lead, tin and other non-ferrous metals, tin content not to exceed 50 percent, having value for re-melting purposes only, in barrels or boxes	55
136080	Residue, zinc lead, in barrels; loose or in packages when shipments weigh 40,000 pounds or more	55
136100	Scrap, antimony metal; in packages, or loose if weighing each 50 pounds or over; loose or in packages when shipments weigh 36,000 pounds or more	60
136120	Scrap, lead base alloy, tin content not exceeding 10 percent, in packages; loose or in packages when shipments weigh 40,000 pounds or more	65
136140	Scrap, NOI, cadmium, in bags, barrels or boxes. See Item 60000 for class dependent upon agreed or released value	85
136160	Scrap, silver plated metal, not on silver, in barrels or boxes, or in machine pressed bales wrapped in burlap	100
136200	Scrap, white metal alloy, NOI; in packages, or loose if weighing each 25 pounds or over; loose or in packages when shipments weigh 40,000 pounds or more	55
136210	Sheet Metal, silver plated, not on silver, NOI, in boxes	150
136220	Shot, britannia metal, in barrels or boxes	70
136240	Silicon, (metal containing not less than 96 percent nor more than 99 percent of silica), in bags, barrels or boxes; loose or in packages when shipments weigh 36,000 pounds or more	50
136260	Silicon Copper, in barrels; loose or in packages when shipments weigh 36,000 pounds or more	70
136340	Silver Plated Ware or Pewter Plated Ware, not on silver or pewter, NOI:	
Sub 1	Not exceeding one inch (2.54 centimeters) in height, in boxes	100
Sub 2	Exceeding one inch (2.54 centimeters) in height, in boxes	150
136380	OSodium, metallic, in steel barrels, in glass in tin cans in boxes, or in metal cans in boxes. See item 60000 for class dependent upon agreed or released value	85
136400	OSodium-potassium Alloys, metallic, in metal containers in wooden boxes	100
136430	Solder, braziers', NOI, other than with gold, palladium or silver content, in barrels or boxes	60
136440	Solder, NOI, other than with gold, palladium or silver content:	
Sub 1	Tin content exceeding 10 percent; in packages, or loose if in pigs or slabs weighing each 25 pounds or over; see Note, item 136441	60
Sub 2	Tin content not exceeding 10 percent:	
Sub 3	Bars, pigs or slabs	55
Sub 4	Other than bars, pigs or slabs, in packages, see Note, item 136441	60
136441	NOTE—Outer shipping package may include one applicator brush for each inner container of solder. Weight of applicator brushes not to exceed 5 percent of the weight of the shipping package.	
136450	Speiss (smelter by-product, containing cobalt-nickel), in bags or barrels; loose or in packages when shipments weigh 50,000 pounds or more	50
136460	Tellurium Metal, in barrels or boxes	100
136470	Terne Ashes, Dross or Skimmings, in double bags, barrels or boxes	55
136480	Terne Metal (alloy of lead and tin), bars, pigs, slabs, or scraps; in packages, or loose if weighing each 25 pounds or over; loose when shipments weigh 36,000 pounds or more	60
136490	Turnings, aluminum and magnesium, mixed, see Note, item 136492, in barrels or boxes	70
136492	NOTE—Applies only on other than scrap turnings. The content of either kind of turning must be not less than 25 percent by weight of the mixture.	
136500	Metal, NOI, or Metal Alloys, NOI:	

Articles, NOI,   Castings,

Bars,   Forgings,

Billets,   Ingots,

Blooms,   Pigs,

(Continued on following page)

For explanation of abbreviations and reference marks, see last page of this tariff. ©ATA 1995

Class Rates

Class rates are those rates that are the basis for most LTL freight moves. It is typically the class rate system that is discounted to provide the rates we normally pay an LTL carrier. We talked about the class rating system at length above and will talk about discounting a little further along.

FAK Rates

FAK (Freight-All-Kinds) rates are a variation on the class rating system. If you ship an assortment of different items with different class ratings, a good strategy is to develop a single class rate under which you can move all of your products. Typically, you will negotiate a low class rating as the basis for your FAK rate. This is a money saver. Then, from an auditing standpoint, it is much easier to audit one class rating rather than multiple ratings. Do this if you have enough volume, and thereby clout, with your carriers.

Point-to-Point Rates

These are usually negotiated on TL shipments. You pay for the capacity of the truck between two named points for a flat charge. The mileage between the two points typically determines them. They are also known as *mileage rates*.

Accessorial Charges

There are a number of *accessorial* (extra) charges a carrier may charge you, over and above the base price. Here are a few of them with a brief explanation of their purpose.

- **Single shipment** - A shipper gives a carrier only one shipment, weighing under 500#, on a given day.
- **Hazardous Materials** - A shipper tenders to a carrier a shipment of some product deemed hazardous by the Department of Transportation (DOT).
- **Detention/Demurrage** - A shipper or consignee makes a carrier wait longer than what the carrier deems customary for loading or unloading a shipment of its size.
- **Notify** - A carrier must set up an appointment for delivery of a shipment.
- **Reconsignment** - A shipper changes the destination of the freight while in-transit.

There are others, but these are some of the more common accessorial charges you may see. The amounts charged for each vary from carrier to carrier and they are negotiable.

Negotiation Strategies

Volume is king, but profitability is queen. This is the cardinal rule of freight negotiation. With a lot of freight volume, you become very attractive to a carrier. However, if moving that freight is not profitable for the carrier, their interest will be lessened. If you have huge volumes of big, bulky lightweight freight which is prone to damage and theft, don't expect to be able to negotiate the same type of pricing as someone with dense, easy to move freight that isn't likely to be broken or stolen. Most carriers are willing to move the freight of a big, national account for little or no profit because these accounts fill-out their trucks, ensuring they don't move empty. The smaller accounts are typically the profit generators for the carriers.

The only thing that you absolutely cannot negotiate is the thing you don't mention. Always negotiate from a position of strength. Know your business. Telling a carrier that you have a lot of freight doesn't help. Have all of your facts and figures together. You should, at minimum, know:

- **Frequency of shipment** - number of shipments per day, week, month, etc.
- **Freight volume** - tonnage shipped or revenue paid to your present carrier for a definite period of time.
- **How quickly you pay your bills** - carriers want to be paid on time. If you are a slow payer, you will be less likely to get a good rate agreement.
- **What is the time your freight will be available for pick-up** - carriers need to see how well you fit into their current schedule.
- **Where are you shipping to and how much volume to each state/region** - carriers need this to determine if your operation fits-in with theirs.
- **Detailed description of the commodity(ies) you are shipping and their respective class ratings** - carriers need to know what they are moving to determine the specific nature of the freight and how economical or costly it will be for them to move it.
- **The percentage of prepaid vs. collect freight** - Prepaid freight is that paid by the shipper. Collect freight is that paid by the consignee. Carrier discounts only apply to the payer of the freight bill. Carriers need to know how much of your freight will be covered by your discount.

There are other factors to consider, and actually, the more information you can provide, the more accurately a carrier can assess your account.

Discounts & Pricing

This is where you get to be the hero. You sit down with one of the multitude of sales representatives that consistently call on you and negotiate a pricing agreement to save your company a ton of money. Okay, so what do you do?

First, you provide to the sales rep the wealth of information you have accumulated on your shipping volumes and shipping lanes. You lay out what your service requirements are so your customers are properly served. Then you ask the rep to submit a proposal. Repeat this process with about three different carriers that can provide the same service. Then evaluate the proposals and pick a winner.

If you have a good amount of volume, try to have all the participating carriers bid off of the same rate base. I see you scratching your head and saying to yourself, huh?

Remember I said that each carrier now develops their own rates. Well comparing the rates of different carriers can be a nightmare. If you can, get them all to bid off of the same set of rates. I use the CF OMNI 555 tariff. You can pick whichever one works for you. If you use the same base rates, then it becomes merely a matter of comparing discount levels. If the rate bases are different, then you have to actually figure out the net rates for each point you ship to, to see who is the least expensive.

A word of warning: do not necessarily pick the cheapest guy in town. I said this earlier and I cannot overemphasize its importance. Choose from reputable carriers that can get the job done. Go to the big guys if you have to. Then, when you are convinced that all of the bidding carriers are equally up to the job, then choose on the basis of price.

Take nothing less than a 50% - 55% discount. These levels are offered to anybody with no volume commitments whatsoever. Push for a 60% discount at minimum. You'll be surprised at what you can get.

Air Transportation

Air transportation is a completely different animal than truck freight. If you are shipping something by airfreight, then there is obviously a critical time factor involved; otherwise you would not be willing to incur the additional cost. If there is one thing about airfreight, it is not cheap, regardless of the carrier. That is not to say that there are not significant cost variations among airfreight providers, but they all are definitely expensive, relative to truck freight.

There are a number of methods for you to use to ship via airfreight. One, is to tender the freight directly to an airline. This can be done through an all cargo airline, such as Federal Express (FedEx), United Parcel Service (UPS), BAX Global, DHL and many others; or with a passenger airline such as American Airlines, TWA, Delta, etc.

The all cargo airlines provide a range of service levels, from next flight out service to a next day or second day delivery. The passenger airlines have over the years looked to sell excess space on their aircraft to the shipping community. Their services though have generally been a second day delivery type of service. If you can live with this type of service level, it can be an economical means of shipping airfreight. Most of our discussion though, will concern itself with next day delivery and even same day delivery. As well, we will largely concern ourselves with the all cargo airlines and freight forwarders as their businesses are tailored specifically towards our needs.

Airlines

The largest all cargo airlines in the United States are Federal Express, United Parcel Service (UPS), Airborne Express, BAX Global and Emery Worldwide. They move freight directly for shippers and they also offer out cargo space to the freight forwarders. The freight is rated on a cost per pound basis and, oftentimes, a distance traveled basis as well. Additionally, the nature of the cargo comes into play in determining the rates, as in the case of truck freight. Bulky, expensive, easily damaged freight is more expensive to ship than dense, low-value and durable freight.

Freight Forwarders

Freight forwarders serve as an intermediary between the airlines and the shipping public. They buy large blocks of space on various airlines, called *pallet positions*, to various locations. They may use both passenger airlines and all cargo airlines. They commit to paying for this space whether it is used or not. As a result, they get an extremely low rate per pound from the airlines. They then resell smaller chunks of this space to individual shippers at a higher rate per pound than they are paying the airline. They also provide pick-up and delivery arrangements, providing a door-to-door service for their customers.

Integrated Carriers

Integrated carriers come in two flavors. First, there is the kind that function as both an airline and freight forwarder. They also will provide complete door-to-door service with their own equipment and personnel. Generally, they own a smaller number of airplanes than an exclusive air carrier, and so, they must make use of the commercial airlines and other all cargo airlines for the volume they cannot handle with their own equipment. BAX and Emery are good examples of this type of integrator.

FedEx and UPS exemplify the other type. In this flavor, the integrator offers the complete package to the shipper. They provide pick-up, the airport-to-airport move and the delivery all on their own equipment, in a completely seamless service.

The differences between the two definitions are subtle and not especially important either.

Next Flight Out Services

Sometimes, a shipment is so critical that it must be delivered the same day you ship it. This type of service is known as *next flight out (NFO)* or *counter-to-counter*. There are a few ways you can make this happen and there are a number of restrictions on what you can ship.

NFO shipments are almost always with the commercial passenger airlines. The freight moves along with the baggage for the flight. Generally, you are restricted to a maximum of between 70 and 100 pounds per shipment. It must be at the airline approximately an hour before the flight departs to ensure it makes that flight.

You can deal directly with the airline or you can use an intermediary. If you deal directly with the airline, you must make arrangements to get the package to the airport and make arrangements for pick-up at destination. You also must find a flight and airline that meets your time requirements. There is a publication called the Official Airline Guide (OAG). This monthly guide lists all domestic flights from all airports to all airports. It is an indispensable tool if you do much NFO shipping.

If this is too much effort for you, many forwarders and integrators offer an NFO service. Simply call a company like Emery or even UPS, through their Sonic Air division, and they will make all the arrangements for you, including pick-up and delivery services. As you can imagine, this is a very expensive service. *Use it sparingly!*

Shipping Documentation

Air Waybill

The air waybill is the airfreight industry's equivalent of the trucking industry's bill of lading. It serves the same general purpose and contains essentially the same information. The forms vary from carrier to carrier, or forwarder to forwarder, but in general, they all ask for the same information. At minimum you should include the following on any air waybill:

- Name and address of shipper.
- Name and address of consignee.
- The gross weight of the shipment.
- An indication of the service level required - next day, second day, etc.
- Who is responsible for the freight charges?

An example of a completed air waybill is provided in figure 9.

Figure 9

EMERY WORLDWIDE A CNF COMPANY

FOR INFORMATION OR RATES
CALL 1-800-HI-EMERY (1-800-443-6379)
http://www.emeryworld.com

DATE OF SHIPMENT: 10/13/98 | ORIGIN: EWR | SHIPMENT NUMBER: 172 683 597 - 9

You Are Making Four Copies. For Legibility, Please Type.

1 FROM - SHIPPER

Shipper's Emery Account Number: C C 1 2 8 9 6 1 1 C

From (Your Name): Charlie Alston
Phone Number (Very Important): 201 434-6778

Company Name: ALPHA METALS
Dept. or Floor: F

Address: 600 ROUTE 440

City: JERSEY CITY
State/Prov.: NJ
Zip/Postal Code (Required): 07304

Shipper's Reference: 592007
First Thirty Characters Will Appear On Invoice

2 TO - CONSIGNEE

Consignee's Emery Account Number:

Contact Name:
Phone Number (Very Important):

Company Name: [illegible] Delco
Dept. or Floor: Plant#XX FM

Address: 4134 Davison Road Dock 43
Emery Cannot Deliver to PO Box or PO Zip Codes

City: Burton
State/Prov.: MI
Zip/Postal Code (Required): 48529

Consignee's Reference: 439101
First Twenty Characters Will Appear On Invoice
Country:

SN- 172 683 597 - 9

NON-NEGOTIABLE AIR WAYBILL 80001-46 (3/97)
LITHO USA EXECUTIVE OFFICES: REDWOOD CITY, CA 94065

SHIPPER'S COPY - 1

3 SERVICES

For Definition of Services See Back of Air Waybill. "X" One Box. *EXTRA CHARGES

U.S., Puerto Rico, & Canada: ☐ *NEXT FLIGHT ☐ SECOND DAY ☐ *09:30 ☐ DEFERRED ☒ AM ☐ *SATURDAY DELIVERY ☐

International: Int'l Door-To-Door: ☐ EXPRESS ☐ STANDARD PLUS; Int'l Airport-To-Airport: ☐ PREFERRED ☐ STANDARD

Preferred and Standard Add'l Services: ☐ *CUSTOMS CLEARANCE REQUESTED ☐ *DELIVERY REQUESTED

4 SHIPMENT DETAILS

Pieces	Length	Width	Height	Description
4	15	12	9	Solder Paste LK721

TOTAL PIECES: 4 | TOTAL WEIGHT: 64 ☒ lbs. ☐ kg. ("X" one) | SKID(S) SAID TO CONTAIN: | TOTAL PIECES:

SPECIAL INSTRUCTIONS:

HANDLING INSTRUCTIONS

*EXTRA CHARGES
+REQUIRES ADVANCE AUTHORIZATION. CALL 1-800-HI-EMERY (1-800-443-6379)

☐ *GOLD PRIORITY+ ☐ *CSS+ ☐ *SSR ☐ ODO+ ☐ DANGEROUS GOODS
☐ HOLD FOR PICKUP ☐ *SPECIAL DELIVERY+ ☐ *INSIDE DELIVERY+ ☐ CONVENTION ☒ PERISHABLE
AUTH/CONF # ☐ OTHER

INTERNATIONAL ONLY

INTERNATIONAL CUSTOMS VALUE (Specify Currency): $
*INTERNATIONAL INSURANCE (Specify Currency): $
CONSIGNEE ID # FOR CUSTOMS (GST/RFC/VAT or as Req'd by Local Customs)
HARMONIZED CODE
COUNTRY OF MANUFACTURE
BROKER NAME/ADDRESS (Use only when International or Canadian Broker requested)
(Unless otherwise specified, Emery Customs Brokers to Clear)
BROKER PHONE NUMBER (Area Code Required)

5 METHOD OF PAYMENT

If No Form of Payment is Checked, the Shipper Shall Be Liable for Charges.

☐ BILL SHIPPER ☒ BILL CONSIGNEE
☐ SHIPPER'S CHECK RECEIVED ☐ FREE DOMICILE (Int'l Only)
Third Party Account Number Mandatory for Third Party Billing
☐ BILL THIRD PARTY EMERY ACCOUNT
☐ GBL (If Character GBL # Required)

6 TERMS AND CONDITIONS

I/we agree that Emery's Terms and Conditions of Contract ("Terms") as set forth on the front and reverse hereof apply to this shipment.

CHECK TO SHIPPER

ONLY IN U.S.A. & CANADA
$

Emery will collect Consignee's check in the amount shown at left, and Shipper assumes all related risks, including, but not limited to, non-payment, fraud and misrepresentation.

DECLARED VALUE AND LIMITS OF LIABILITY

DECLARED VALUE: $ 1372

EMERY'S LIABILITY SHALL BE LIMITED TO THE HIGHER OF $50.00 PER SHIPMENT OR $0.50 PER POUND OF CARGO LOST OR DAMAGED, UNLESS YOU SPECIFY A HIGHER AMOUNT IN THE DECLARED VALUE BOX. EMERY SHALL IN NO EVENT BE LIABLE FOR ANY SPECIAL, INCIDENTAL OR CONSEQUENTIAL DAMAGES. IF THIS SHIPMENT INVOLVES INTERNATIONAL TRANSPORTATION, EMERY'S LIABILITY SHALL BE LIMITED TO $9.07 PER POUND OF CARGO LOST OR DAMAGED UNLESS YOU SPECIFY A HIGHER AMOUNT IN THE DECLARED VALUE BOX AND THE WARSAW CONVENTION MAY GOVERN AND THEREBY LIMIT OUR LIABILITY.

For International and Canadian shipments, Exporter understands that commercial invoices and other special documents may be required, and authorizes Emery to act as Forwarding Agent for export control and customs purposes.

Time Rec'd	Date Rec'd	Route No.	Employee ID #

GOODS REC'D AT: ☐ Shipper's Door ☐ Service Center ☐ Carrier Advance ☐ Convention ☐ Residence ☐

SHIPPER'S AUTHORIZATION AND SIGNATURE
X ______ Date: ______

Rate Development & Negotiation

Airfreight rates are a much simpler affair than LTL truck rates. Once a carrier or forwarder understands your products and their freight characteristics, and the lanes you ship to, they will provide you with one of two different rate structures - a single-zone rate structure or a multi-zone rate structure. Our discussion of these different approaches follows below.

Single Zone Rates

A single zone rate structure, as its name implies, provides a single, flat rate per pound to any destination in the U.S., regardless of the distance you are shipping. So, if you are shipping 100# from New York City to Los Angeles, it would cost you the same as if you shipped 100# from New York City to Columbus, OH. The premise behind this is simplicity and the law of averages. If you ship all over the country, the fact that you are paying the same for a long-distance as you would for a short-distance all evens out in the long run. The primary advantage to this method is simplicity. It is much easier to deal with one rate as opposed to five or six.

Multi-Zone Rates

Multi-zone rates, as their name indicates, provide different rates per pound depending upon the distance traveled. The carrier or forwarder divides the country into zones and charges more for longer distance moves than shorter distance ones. The advantage to this method is that if you ship predominantly short distances, you can save a good amount of money. However, if you primarily ship long distances, the cost can kill you. Also, it is more complex than single zone rates because you are dealing with five or six different rates per pound dependent upon the zone.

UPS and FedEx recently converted from single zone rates to multi-zone. I don't like it, but that is because my airfreight is pretty evenly distributed across the country. This is a personal decision you need to make dependent upon your traffic lanes. With most forwarders, the rate structure is negotiable.

Dimensional Weight

Airlines do not like to move big, bulky freight. They want nice, dense freight. If you have light, bulky freight they will charge you extra for it. This is called *dimensionalizing* or *dimming*. Carriers have a formula for calculating what the weight of a piece of freight should be based upon its dimensions. It is typically calculated as follows:

(Length in inches X width in inches X height in inches) / 194 = dimensional weight. (The **194** is called the dim factor. It is pretty standard in the industry).

If your piece of freight weighs less than the dimensional weight, they will charge you for the dim weight. It does not work both ways however. If your freight weighs more than its dim weight, they will not charge you the dim weight. You will be charged the actual weight. For those of you who ship Styrofoam cups, you are in trouble.

Negotiation Strategies

The approach to negotiating airfreight agreements is essentially the same as that for motor freight. You must have all your ducks in a row before you sit down with a sales rep, otherwise they will be unable to accurately assess the level of business they can expect to receive.

Remember that everything is negotiable; so don't be shy to ask for a concession. If you can, try to eliminate any *beyond charges*. These are extra charges assessed for shipments to points that are of considerable distance from an airport. They are usually quite negotiable. Also, if you have any sort of significant airfreight volume, you should not pay more that $1.00 per pound on shipments weighing over 100# with any freight forwarder. If you are, then you may be giving away more than you have to.

Small Package Carriers

Small package carriers are those that move packages ranging in size from a letter to 150#. Depending upon the carrier, they can be moved either by a ground service or by air. The ground services of UPS and FedEx Ground are an extremely economical means of moving freight. The air services are generally rather expensive on a cost per pound basis.

United Parcel Service (UPS)

United Parcel Service (UPS) is the world's largest transportation company, moving approximately 12,000,000 packages per day. That's a lot of freight! The company offers to the shipping community a broad range of domestic products: guaranteed ground service, 3 Day Select, 2nd Day Air, 2nd Day Air AM, Next Day Saver (PM delivery), Next Day Air (AM delivery), Next Day Air Early AM (8:00 am delivery), and Sonic Air (same day delivery). They provide a selection of international products as well.

Their rates are constructed on a multi-zone basis with the cost predicated upon the weight and the distance traveled. The company offers a number of value-added services to the shipper above and beyond the actual transportation. They have an Internet Web site located at www.ups.com from where you can trace packages, order supplies or make shipments. As well, UPS will provide to shippers with sufficient volume a PC based automated shipping system - *free-of-charge*. This is known as **UPS Online Professional**. It is a very nice Microsoft Windows-based system.

Federal Express (FedEx)

Started in 1974 as the outgrowth of an MBA project prepared by company founder and CEO Fred Smith, FedEx is the world's largest express package company moving about 4 million packages per day. They have grown dramatically over the years by adding different products and acquiring compatible competitors. In the 1980s, FedEx acquired Flying Tigers, the world's largest all cargo airline at the time. Recently, FedEx bought Caliber Systems. Caliber was the parent company for RPS, Roberts Express, Viking Freight and Caliber Logistics. In 2000, they bought the LTL carrier American Freightways.

The company offers varying levels of service including same day, next day, second day, heavy weight and assorted international services. They also offer to qualified shippers, *free-of-charge*, their **Powership** PC-based shipping systems. Like UPS, they offer an assortment of value-added services through their Internet Web site at www.fedex.com.

FedEx Ground (RPS)

RPS started back in 1984 as an alternative to UPS' ground service. The company began as a division of Roadway Express - the LTL carrier. Hence, the name stood for Roadway Package System. Since then, Roadway spun-off some of its divisions and RPS is now owned by Federal Express. In early 2000, FedEx changed the company's name to FedEx Ground.

FedEx Ground's base ground service rates are the same as that of UPS. However, they tend to be more aggressive in offering discounts than UPS. From a service standpoint, I feel more comfortable with UPS than FedEx Ground, but that is only a personal opinion. Overall, their ground service is quite good.

Declared Value

Most small package carriers offer package insurance to the shipper. The first $100 of value is insured for free. For every increment of $100 above that, the carrier will charge anywhere between $.35 and $.50 per $100 or fraction thereof. On high value shipments, this can get quite expensive. There are some third-party parcel insurance companies on the market that charge considerably less. Some of the better-known providers of this type of service are:

- Parcel Insurance Plan (PIP)
- Universal Parcel Insurance
- Neopost Parcel Coverage

This is a good strategy to pursue should you ship a large amount of high value goods.

Expedited Carriers

These carriers fill a niche between regular LTL motor freight and airfreight. If you have a time critical shipment that cannot be satisfied through the service level provided by LTL carriers, and you do not want to go for the expense of airfreight, these are the type of guys you want to go to. Some carriers will pinpoint delivery times to within a two-hour window. The way many of these services work is, you talk to a customer service rep, tell them the size of your shipment, where you are located and where it is going. They will then come back to you with a price and a transit time. If both elements meet your needs, you are good to go. This service does not come cheap. But, in most cases it will cost you less than airfreight so it is a viable alternative.

Time-Definite Services

The premier carrier in this market is FedEx Custom Critical (formerly Roberts Express). They have been providing time-definite services for a long time and have it down to a science. They offer a wide array of equipment to handle almost any size shipment, anywhere. You can even charter an aircraft through them. Roberts Express became a part of FedEx through the Caliber Systems acquisition. In the early part of 2000, they were re-branded with the FedEx name along with RPS. They can provide support 24 hours per day, 365 days per year.

Deferred Airfreight

Many freight forwarders offer what is known as deferred airfreight. This is typically a three to five day service anywhere in the country. The name is misleading though because generally, the freight is not flown, it is trucked. The freight forwarder hooks-up with an owner-operator heading in the direction of the load and matches the load to the equipment. This is a very nice type of service if it meets with your needs.

Specialty Carriers

Specialty carriers are those that handle freight requiring special equipment, namely that which the traditional LTL carrier typically does not provide. This may include freight shipped in bulk; large, difficult to handle freight; or freight requiring particular climatic conditions.

Bulk Carriers

The most readily recognizable bulk carrier would be one operating tankers. Used for moving anything from hazardous chemicals, to heating oil to food grade products, they are a common sight on the nation's highways.

Heavy Haul Carriers

These carriers can move a broad range of bulky or difficult to handle freight. There is a variety of equipment used to move the myriad of freight that can be offered to them. Some of the more common configurations are:

- Flat-bed
- Step-deck or drop-deck
- Double drop-deck
- Detachable goose-neck

I have included an illustration of the various types of equipment available in figure 10.

Temperature Controlled Carriers

Due to the nature of some products, temperature controlled trailers are required to ensure the integrity of the goods upon delivery. Some products, primarily food, require refrigeration. This equipment is known in the industry as a *reefer*.

Other commodities, such as some chemicals, require protect from freezing *(PFF)*. For this type of service, heated trailers are necessary.

There are specific carriers that offer these services. C.R. England is a well-known reefer carrier and Jevic Transportation provides a good heated service.

Inter-Modal

Inter-modal services make use of both motor freight and rail freight to effect delivery. Freight will be loaded in a trailer or ocean container and delivered to the nearest rail yard. The container or trailer is then loaded on a rail flat car, moved to another rail yard near the destination, off-loaded, hooked-up to another truck and then delivered to its final destination. This is normally a slower process than standard truck service, but the cost saving can be significant. A full coast-to-coast truckload can cost about $2,500, whereas

Figure 10

4 Axle Lowboy Trailer

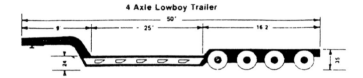

Extendable Flatbed Trailer

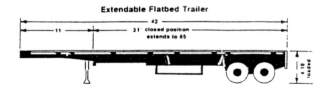

Single Drop Trailer

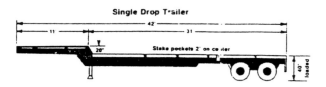

Extendable Single Drop Trailer

Double Drop Trailer

Detachable Gooseneck Lowboy Trailer

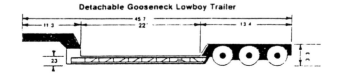

2-5 Axle Lowboy Trailer

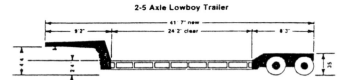

Extendable Double Drop Lowboy Trailer

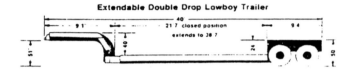

Double Drop Removable Gooseneck Lowboy Trailer

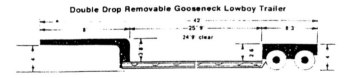

shipping the same quantity as an inter-modal move may cost you approximately $1,600. The transit time by truck will probably be about four days, while the inter-modal move will take about six days. If you have full-loads and you can live with the transit time, this is a great money-saving alternative.

This type of service can also be known as **piggyback**, trailer-on-flat-car **(TOFC)** or container-on-flat-car **(COFC)**.

Freight Terms, Liabilities & Responsibilities

This is a crucial aspect of transportation and logistics because it has to do with your money. If you don't properly handle these transactions, you could wind-up paying for something you shouldn't.

Collect vs. Prepaid

These are two of the most common terms in transportation. These words indicate who is responsible for paying the carrier's freight bill. You had better make sure that you do this correctly or you may be in for a big surprise.

Collect indicates that the freight is payable by the consignee or recipient of the freight. *Prepaid* means that the shipper of the goods is responsible for paying the freight charges. It is very simple, *but very important*.

A variation on this is something called *prepay and add*. This method entails the shipper paying the carrier for the freight charges and then the shipper invoices the customer for the freight. This is done for various reasons. One, a shipper may have very good discounts with a carrier and the consignee would like to take advantage of them. Or, the consignee may just not want to deal with the carrier and work exclusively with the shipper. *If you ship prepay and add, make sure you invoice your customer!!!*

Rather than having the freight bill sent to either the shipper or the consignee, the freight may be billed to a third-party. For example, if you are a catalog house, and you ship from various distributors and manufacturers, you may have your distributor make you responsible for the freight by indicating on the bill of lading to bill you. In this way, the distributor does not pay the freight nor does the consignee, but the third party catalog house will pay the carrier. In the body of the bill of lading, clearly indicate: *Bill Third Party* and include that party's name and address.

Cash on Delivery (COD)

If you do not trust the creditworthiness of your customer, you may use your carrier as a collection agent for you. Indicate on the bill of lading, in the COD block, the dollar amount of the goods you are shipping, and the carrier will not deliver the freight unless they receive a check from the consignee. The carrier then sends the check to you. The carriers charge for this service, but it is nominal and sometimes well worth it.

Free on Board (FOB) Terms

The *FOB* terms (pronounced eff-oh-bee), indicate the way in which a product has been sold to a customer. As mentioned above, the abbreviation stands for free on board and reflects the loading of freight onto a carrier's piece of equipment.

The FOB terms represent a number of different factors concerning how a sale is made. These terms cover:

- Who pays the freight?
- Where is the place of delivery?
- Where is title and control of the goods passed?
- Where is the shipping point?
- How is the total cost to be determined?
- When is payment due?
- Who pays for packaging?
- Who selects the carrier and arranges for transport?
- Who is responsible for the cost of loading the carrier's equipment?
- Who absorbs the risk of transportation? (Morse, pp. 111-112)

FOB applies in both international and domestic shipping, although in international sales, the international standard called *Incoterms* has largely replaced the older FOB designations.

There are six basic FOB designations. The most common in domestic transportation are FOB Origin and FOB Destination. We will explain all six individually as they significantly affect who is responsible for the freight charges, where the title to the goods passes, and who has responsibility for loss and damage claims.

1. FOB Origin - The title passes at origin (shipper's dock) and the consignee is responsible for the freight charges. The freight is shipped on a collect basis.
2. FOB Origin, Freight Prepaid - Same as #1 only the shipper pays the freight.
3. FOB Origin, Freight Prepaid and Charged Back - Same as #1, but the shipper pays the carrier for the freight and then invoices the consignee for the freight charges.
4. FOB Destination - The title passes at destination (consignee's dock) and the shipper is responsible for the freight charges. The freight is shipped on a prepaid basis.
5. FOB Destination, Freight Collect - Same as #4 only the consignee pays the freight.
6. FOB Destination, Freight Collect and Allowed - Same as #4, but the consignee pays the carrier for the freight charges and then deducts those charges from the seller's invoice for the goods. (Southern, pp. 167-168)

For a larger company, you should always specify FOB Origin as your purchase terms on inbound freight. That way, you will get the benefit of using your carriers and paying the advantageous rates you have negotiated. Ensure that your purchasing department specifies the correct terms of sale on any purchase order they issue, and also stipulates the appropriate carrier to use. This can save you a great deal of money.

Claims

Overcharge Claims

As I mentioned earlier, carriers of all modes are known to make mistakes when billing their freight charges. It is *your* responsibility to ensure that your company does not pay more than they should for any shipment. *Audit* (check) your freight bills for accuracy. Demand from your carriers a copy of the bill of lading to accompany all outbound prepaid shipment freight bills. Stipulate, as well, that your carriers submit a signed copy of the delivery receipt to accompany all inbound collect shipment freight bills. This substantiates that the shipments actually occurred and allows you to compare the information on the support documentation against that of the freight bill. You would be amazed at the discrepancies sometimes!

Get a PC for your department and have your carriers provide their rates to you on diskette. Then you can accurately assess whether or not you are being invoiced correctly. If you find an error, file an overcharge with the carrier and recover what is due you. The statute of limitations on filing overcharge claims is *180 days* from time of shipment.

Some of the more common errors made by carriers in their invoicing process include:

- Description of product.
- Weight of shipment.
- Arithmetic mistake.
- Duplicate invoicing.
- Wrong payment terms - prepaid vs. collect.
- Incorrect rate.
- Incorrect class rating.
- Incorrect discount level.

Please be on the lookout for any or all of these!

Loss & Damage Claims

I hope this is an area where you never gain a whole lot of hands-on experience. No one wants to deal with the loss or damage of a shipment. Unfortunately, however, it does happen. And when it does you need to know what to do to protect the interests of your company.

A carrier's liability is limited to either the actual value of the goods or some released value for that commodity specified in the National Motor Freight Classification (NMFC).

The general rule of loss and damage claims is:

1. The party with title to the goods is the party responsible for filing a claim.
2. The claim may be filed against either the originating carrier or the delivering carrier (if there is a difference).
3. Claims must be filed within nine months of delivery.
4. If the carrier declines the claim, the claimant has two years from the date of denial in which to file a lawsuit.
5. The claimant and carrier may jointly agree to submit the claim to arbitration through the Transportation Arbitration Board.
6. The claimant may file for the actual loss, which means the amount, which will fully compensate the claimant for his loss.
7. Concealed loss or damage claims must be filed within 15 calendar days from date of delivery. Ensure the cargo is maintained in its original condition while awaiting assessment. The burden of proof is on the claimant to prove loss or damage in transit.
8. The carrier is not liable for:
   - Acts of God.
   - Acts of the public enemy.
   - Acts of public authority.
   - Acts of the shipper.
   - The inherent nature of the goods.
9. The burden of proof is on the carrier. (Southern, pp. 120-122)

I know I mentioned this earlier, but I cannot overemphasize its importance. If you receive damaged freight, you must note the damage on the delivery receipt. If you cannot fully ascertain the extent of the damage at time of delivery, merely state that "the degree of the damage is unknown at this time, the goods are subject to later inspection." Ensure that you keep a copy of this delivery receipt. You will need it when you file the claim. A ***Standard Form for Presentation of Loss and Damage Claims*** is included in figure 11.

Hazardous Materials Transportation

Hazardous materials transportation is a complex, highly regulated process that requires formalized training and strict compliance with the applicable regulations. There are countless books devoted solely to this subject and I won't even attempt to scratch the surface here. My intent is just to make you aware of the magnitude of the regulations and stress the importance of compliance.

STANDARD FORM FOR PRESENTATION OF LOSS AND DAMAGE CLAIM
(Read Instructions on Back Before Filling Out This Form)

To: _____
(Name of Carrier)

_____
(Street Address)

_____
(City, State)

_____
(Date)

_____
(Claimant's Number)

_____
(Carrier's Number)

This Claim for $_____ is made against your company for ☐ Damage ☐ Loss in connection with the following describes shipment:

_____ *(Shipper's Name)*	_____ *(Consignee's Name)*
_____ *(Point Shipped From)*	_____ *(Final Destination)*
_____ *(Name of Carrier Issuing Bill of Lading)*	_____ *(Name of Delivering Carrier)*
_____ *(Date of Bill of Lading)*	_____ *(Date of Delivery)*
_____ *(Routing of Shipment)*	_____ *(Delivering Carrier's Freight Bill No.)*

If shipment reconsigned en route, state particulars: _____

If shipment moved from warehousing or distribution point, indicate name of initial shipper and point of origin, and, if known, name of prior carrier or carriers and prior billing references: _____

Detailed Statement Showing How Amount Claimed is Determined
(Number and description of articles, nature and extent loss or damage, invoice price of articles, amount of claim, etc.
ALL DISCOUNT and ALLOWANCES MUST BE SHOWN.)

NMFC Item No. of commodity lost or damaged _____	Total Amount Claimed

The following documents are submitted in support of this claim:
☐ Original Bill of Lading.
☐ Original paid freight bill or other carrier document bearing notation of loss or damage if not shown on freight bill.
☐ Carrier's Inspection Report Form (Concealed loss or damage).
☐ Consignee concealed loss or damage form.
☐ Original invoice or certified copy.
☐ Shipper's concealed loss or damage form.
☐ Other particulars obtainable in proof of loss or damage Claimed:

(Note: The absence of any document called for in connection with this claim must be explained. When impossible for claimant to produce original bill of lading, or paid freight bill, a bond of indemnity must be given to protect carrier against duplicate claim supported by original documents.)

_____
(Claimants Name)

_____
(Address)

A.T.A. Standard Form No. F.C.S. 18

Printed by AMERICAN TRUCKING ASSOCIATIONS, INC. 1616 "P" Street N.W., Washington, D.C. 20036 U.S.A.

Figure 11

Before you ship any hazardous materials, you must be formally trained. There are a number of sources for this training. Unz &Co., Lion Technology and some of the carriers hold seminars at locations around the country. They usually last from two to three whole days. To remain in compliance, you must be re-certified every three years. If you ship haz-mat, and you are not formally trained, stop what you are doing and get trained immediately. There is both corporate and personal liability involved here if it is discovered that you are not complying with the law.

Each mode of transport has its own governing body to worry about. The Department of Transportation (DOT) regulates domestic motor freight. Airfreight has the International Civil Aviation Organization (ICAO) as its governing body. The International Maritime Organization (IMO) regulates ocean freight. Each mode has its own regulations. Motor freight has the Code of Federal Regulations, Title 49 (49 CFR). The International Air Transport Association (IATA) publishes the ICAO Technical Instructions for the regulation of air transport. And ocean freight uses the International Maritime Dangerous Goods (IMDG) Code. There are many similarities among the regulations, but there are some differences of which you must be aware.

There are nine major classes of hazardous materials:

Class 1 - Explosives
Class 2 - Gases
Class 3 - Flammable Liquids
Class 4 - Flammable Solids/Spontaneously Combustible/Dangerous When Wet
Class 5 - Oxidizers/Organic Peroxides
Class 6 - Poisons/Infectious Substances
Class 7 - Radioactives
Class 8 - Corrosives
Class 9 - Miscellaneous

Everything associated with haz-mat is regulated: the shipping documents, labeling, packaging, marking, etc. Do not ignore the regulatory requirements. For one, it could cause a disaster costing people their lives and property. Second, you ***personally***, and/or your company, could face civil or criminal penalties up to and including imprisonment.

Shipping dangerous goods is a very precise process and I hate to treat it summarily, yet if I were to deal with it fully, it would require a volume as large as the complete work. So to finish-up treatment of this very important topic, I'll leave you with some examples of what a completed haz-mat package looks like (figure 12), some sample documentation (figure 13) and a quick look at some hazard package labels (Figure 14).

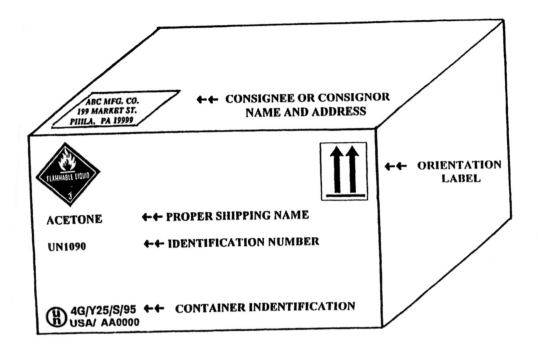

Figure 12

SHIPPER'S DECLARATION FOR DANGEROUS GOODS

Shipper	Air Waybill No. 800 1234 5686
ABC Company 1000 High Street Youngsville, Ontario Canada	Page 1 of 1 Pages Shipper's Reference Number (optional)

Consignee	
CBA Ltd 50 Rue de la Paix Paris 75 006 France	For optional use for Company logo name and address

Two completed and signed copies of this Declaration must be handed to the operator.

WARNING

TRANSPORT DETAILS

This shipment is within the limitations prescribed for: (delete non-applicable)	Airport of Departure: Youngsville
~~PASSENGER AND CARGO AIRCRAFT~~ CARGO AIRCRAFT ONLY	

Airport of Destination: Paris, Charles de Gaulle

Failure to comply in all respects with the applicable Dangerous Goods Regulations may be in breach of the applicable law, subject to legal penalties. This Declaration must not, in any circumstances, be completed and/or signed by a consolidator, a forwarder or an IATA cargo agent.

Shipment type: (delete non-applicable)
NON-RADIOACTIVE ~~RADIOACTIVE~~

NATURE AND QUANTITY OF DANGEROUS GOODS

Proper Shipping Name	Class or Division	UN or ID No.	Packing Group	Subsidiary Risk	Quantity and type of packing	Packing Inst.	Authorization
Nicotine	6.1	UN1654	II		1 Steel drum 20 L	611	
Self-reactive solid type D (Benzene Sulphohydrazide)	4.1	UN3226	II		1 Fibreboard box x 10 kg	430	
Paint	3	UN1263	II		2 Fibreboard boxes x 4 L	305	
Paints	3	UN1263	III		1 Fibreboard box 30 L	309	
Vehicle (flammable liquid powered)	9	UN3166			One automobile 1350 kg	900	
Chemical kits	9	UN3316	II		1 Fibreboard box x 3 kg	915	

Additional Handling Information

The packages containing UN3226 must be shaded from direct sunlight, stored away from all sources of heat in a well ventilated area and not overstowed with other cargo.

I hereby declare that the contents of this consignment are fully and accurately described above by the proper shipping name, and are classified, packaged, marked and labelled/placarded, and are in all respects in proper condition for transport according to applicable international and national governmental regulations.	Name/Title of Signatory B. Smith, Dispatch Supervisor Place and Date Youngsville 1 January 1999 Signature (see warning above) B. Smith

Figure 13

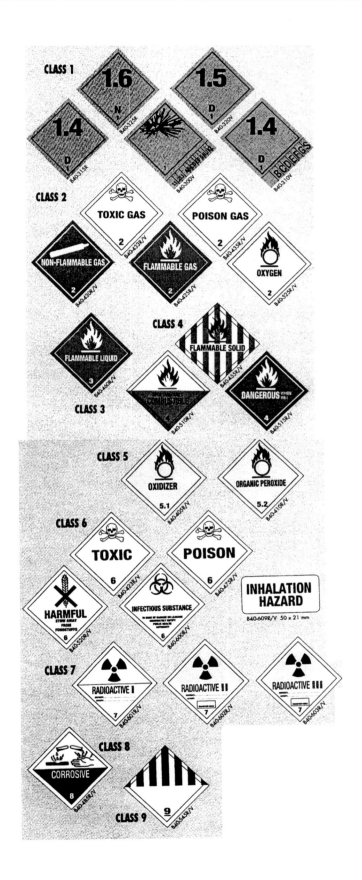

Figure 14

Chapter 2

International Transportation

International transportation, while using the same modes of transport as domestic transportation, adds ocean freight as another common means of transport. The primary difference, from an operational standpoint, between domestic and international transportation is the documentation requirements associated with international trade. Because the freight is leaving the commerce of the United States and entering that of another country, certain specific documents are required to enable the freight to move.

Governments want to track their exports, so, as in the case of the United States; a Shipper's Export Declaration must be prepared in many cases by the shipper so our government can get a handle on what and where we export. Countries want to collect revenue from importers based upon what they import. This revenue is called **duty**. In order to calculate duty, the government must know the description and value of the imported goods. This is done through a commercial invoice. In addition to these documents, other documents are required for various reasons. We will cover them all, and their purposes, as we go forward.

Overview of the International Transportation Scene

What complicates international transportation and trade is the fact that you are doing business between two different countries. Each country has their own set of rules and regulations when you try to do business with them. The process is really quite straightforward; it is just a matter of learning the documentary requirements of each country and how to properly prepare those documents.

Please note, if you do not prepare the documents correctly or omit a necessary document, you could either cost someone a lot of extra money or prevent the transaction from happening. If you do not provide what a government requires, your goods could be seized and impounded. You definitely don't want that to happen.

So if your company is involved in international trade and you have responsibility for the logistics piece of the pie, please pay close attention to the material that follows. *If you do this incorrectly, you could be in for a world of headaches*.

The Export Process

The primary issue associated with exporting revolves around meeting the documentary requirements of the country to which you are shipping. In the following, we will discuss in depth the various documents you may need and the information they must contain.

Documentation

There are two kinds of documentation you may need to properly execute an export - U.S. Government requirements and foreign government requirements. We will talk about the U.S. Government's needs first, as they are the simplest.

The U.S. Government, for most exports, requires only one document - the *Shipper's Export Declaration*. This is commonly referred to as an export dec or *SED*. The government uses the data collected from this document to assess what, how much and to where we export. In figure 15 you will see a completed Shipper's Export Declaration.

In general, it is required for any export made from the United States. With that being said, there are a number of notable exemptions from filing of which you should be aware. Some of the more significant include:

- The value of each classification is less than $2,500.00 and an export license is not required.
- Shipments to the U.S. Armed Services.
- Shipments to U.S. Government Agencies and employees.
- Shipments to Canada that do not require an export license.

Foreign governments may require an assortment of documents. We will look at the most common ones. Every country requires a *commercial invoice* of some sort. This is the primary document used in international trade. This document contains, at minimum, the name and address of the shipper, the name and address of the consignee, a description of the goods and the price at which they are being sold. Other pieces of significant information should be included as well. In figure 16, I have a completed commercial invoice with all the necessary information included.

This is the document that a government will use to assess duty on an imported commodity. It is most important that the information contained on the invoice be as correct as possible. If it is wrong, it could cost your customer extra money in duties or delay the delivery of their shipment.

U.S. DEPARTMENT OF COMMERCE - U.S. CENSUS BUREAU -Economics and Statistics Administration - BUREAU OF EXPORT ADMINISTRATION

Form 7525-V (7-25-2000) **SHIPPER'S EXPORT DECLARATION** OMB No. 0607-0152

1a. U.S. PRINCIPAL PARTY IN INTEREST (USPPI) *(Complete name and address)*			
Fictitious Solder Company, Inc. 123 Park Avenue New York, NY	ZIP CODE 10001	2.DATE OF EXPORTATION 4/6/01	3.TRANSPORTATION REFERENCE NO. 000-1234 5678

b. USPPI EIN (IRS) OR ID NO. 12-3456789	c. PARTIES TO TRANSACTION ☐ Relate ☑ Non-Related

4a. ULTIMATE CONSIGNEE *(Complete name and address)*
Asia Electronics KK
123 Yokohama Street
Tokyo

Japan

b.INTERMEDIATE CONSIGNEE *(Complete name and address)*

5. FORWARDING AGENT *(Complete name and address)* Danzas AEI Cargo Building 89 Jamaica, NY 11430	6. POINT (STATE) OF ORIGIN OR FTZ NO. New York	7. COUNTRY OF ULTIMATE DESTINATION Japan

8. LOADING PIER *(vessel only)*	9. METHOD OF TRANSPORTATION *(specify)* Air	14. CARRIER IDENTIFICATION CODE: JAL-JAPAN AIRLINES COMPA	15. SHIPMENT REFERENCE NO. 2001
10. EXPORTING CARRIER JAL	11. PORT OF EXPORT 4701-JOHN F. KENNEDY AIRPOR	16. ENTRY NUMBER	17. HAZARDOUS MATERIALS ☐ Yes ☑ No
12. PORT OF UNLOADING *(vessel and air only)* 58886-TOKYO,JAPAN	13. CONTAINERIZED *(vessel only)* ☐ Yes ☑ No	18. IN BOND CODE	19. ROUTED EXPORT TRANSACTION ☐ Yes ☑ No

20. SCHEDULE B DESCRIPTION OF COMMODITIES *(Use Columns 22-24)*					
D/F or M (21)	Schedule B Number (22)	QUANTITY-SCHEDULE B UNITS (23)	SHIPPING WEIGHT (Kilograms) (24)	VIN/PRODUCT NUMBER/VEHICLE TITLE NUMBER (25)	VALUE (U.S. dollars, omit cents) (Selling price or cost if not sold) (26)
D	Solder 8311.30.3000	1200 lbs	589.7		$3,000
D	Flux 3810.90.0000	110 Gal	453.6		$2,750

27. LICENSE NO./LICENSE EXCEPTION SYMBOL/AUTHORIZATION NLR	28. ECCN (when required) EAR99
29. Duly authorized officer or employee E.X. Porter	The USPPI authorizes the forwarder named above to act as forwarding agent for export control and customs purposes.

30. I certify that all statements made and all information contained herein are true and correct and that I have read and understand the instructions for preparation of this document, set forth in the "Correct Way to Fill Out the Shipper's Export Declaration." I understand that civil and criminal penalties, including forfeiture and sale, may be imposed for making false or fraudulent statements herein, failing to provide the requested information or for violation of U.S laws on exportation (13 U.S.C. Sec 306; 22 U.S.C. Sec. 401; 18 U.S.C. Sec. 1001; 50 U.S.C. App. 2410).

Signature *E. X. Porter*	Confidential—For use solely for official purposes authorized by the Secretary of Commerce (13 U.S.C 301 (g)).
Title Manager	Export shipments are subject to inspection by U.S. Customs Service and/or Office of Export Enforcement.
Date 4/6/01	31. Authentification *(When Required)*
Telephone No. *(Include Area Code)* (212) 555-1212	E-mail address exporter@fictitioussolder.com

Figure 15

Commercial Invoice

Exporter:
Fictitious Solder Company, Inc.
123 Park Avenue
New York, NY 10001

Date: 00/11/19

PO Number: 987654

Order Number: 34567

Terms: Collect

Ultimate Consignee:
Asia Electronics KK
123 Yokahama Street
Tokyo
Japan

Commercial Invoice Number: 123/00

Pro Forma Invoice Number: 24580

Consignee Phone Number:

Customer Account Number: 5678

Intermediate Consignee:

Exporting Carrier: JAL

Loading Pier/Terminal: JFK Airport

Point of Origin (FTZ No.): New York

Ultimate Destination: Japan

Pieces:	Units:	Product Description:	Product ID:	Product Name:	Marks:	Harmonized Code:	Unit Price:	Value:
55	Gal	Flux	67890	Flux	Asia Electronics KK	3810.90	$1.00	$55.00
1000	lbs	Solder	12345	Solder	Asia Electronics KK	8311.30	$2.50	$2,500.00

SAMPLE

These commodities, technology or software were exported from the United States in accordance with the Export Administration Regulations. Diversion contrary to U.S. law prohibited.

Ex-Works Value: $2,555.00

Other Charges:

Total: EXW New York $2,555.00
USD

Title: Manager

Authorized Signature: Ex Porter

Figure 16

A variation on the commercial invoice is the **Canada Customs Invoice**. This is a document required by the government of Canada in lieu of a commercial invoice. It is not required all of the time. There are certain exemptions. Primarily, if the value of the shipment is under $1,600.00 Canadian, then a standard commercial invoice may be used. It contains most of the same information as a plain, old commercial invoice, but there are a few other pieces of information requested as well. I have included a completed Canada Customs Invoice in figure 17.

As long as we are discussing Canada, we might as well discuss the **North American Free Trade Agreement (NAFTA) Certificate of Origin** next. A certificate of origin attests to the country of origin (manufacture) of the goods. Most countries have different duty rates on goods dependent upon the country of origin. The United States, Canada and Mexico entered into a treaty to phase-out all duties on goods moving between the three countries. The catch though is that the goods must be made in one of the three countries. This document, the NAFTA Certificate of Origin, certifies that the goods shipped are made in one of these three countries. If you are shipping something made in another country to Canada or Mexico, then the form is not used. In that case, use a standard certificate of origin. I have a sample, completed NAFTA Certificate of Origin in figure 18.

For most other countries, a standard **certificate of origin** is useable. Again, this form attests to the country of manufacture of the goods you are shipping. It should be considered a standard document to use for all exports, regardless of the country of destination. I have included a standard certificate of origin in figure 19.

Another common document is called a **packing list**. This document specifies what you are shipping, how it is marked and packaged, and the weights and dimensions of the goods. It is important for the consignee from a handling and receiving perspective. A sample completed packing list is provided in figure 20.

On occasion, a customer in a foreign country may need to obtain an import license in order to import your product into his country. To be able to do this, he must be able to provide to his government officials a complete description of the anticipated import transaction. The document used for this purpose is called a **Proforma Invoice**. Its other major uses are as a quotation for a potential purchase or as a substitute for a missing commercial invoice. A completed proforma invoice is provided in figure 21.

Another document you will use, although it is not a governmental requirement, is called a **Shipper's Letter of Instruction (SLI)**. This provides information to an international freight forwarder so they can correctly ship your cargo for you. Figure 22 contains a completed Shipper's Letter of Instruction.

These are the most common documents you will encounter in a typical export operation. Of course, there are others, but again, I am trying to deal with the generalities and not the

CANADA CUSTOMS INVOICE
FACTURE DES DOUANES CANADIENNES

Revenue Canada
Customs and excise

1. Vendor (Name and Address)/Vendeur (Nom et adresse)	2. Date of Direct Shipment to Canada/Date d'expédition directe vers le Canada
Fictitious Solder Company, Inc. 123 Park Avenue New York, NY 10001	11/19/2000

| 3. Other References (Include Purchaser's Order No.)
Autres références (Inclure le n° de commande de l'acheteur)

45-9876 |

| 4. Consignee (Name and Address)/Destinataire (Nom et adresse)

Canada Electronics, Inc.
123 Rue de Canada
Montreal, Quebec J2L 1E3
Canada | 5. Purchaser's Name and Address (If other than Consignee)
Nom et adresse de l'acheteur (S'il diffère du destinataire) |

| 6. Country of Transhipment/Pays de transbordement |

7. Country of Origin of Goods/Pays d'origine des merchandises	If shipment includes goods of different origin, enter origins against items 12. Si l'expédition comprend des marchandises d'origines différentes, préciser leur presence en 12
USA	

| 8. Transportation: Give Mode and Place of Direct Shipment to Canada
Transport: Préciser mode et point d'expédition direct vers le canada
Truck

Consolidated Freightways | 9. Conditions of Sale and Terms of Payment (i.e. Sale, Consignment Shipment, Leased Goods, etc.)
Conditions de vente et modalités de paiement (p. ex. vente, expédition en consignation, location de marchandises, etc.)
Sale - Net 15 Days |

10. Currency of Settlement/Devises du paiement
US Dollars

11. No. of Pkgs/Nbre de colis	12. Specification of Commodities (Kind of Packages, Marks and Numbers, General Description and Characteristics, i.e. Grade, Quality) - Désignation des articles (Nature des colis, marques et numéros, description générale et caractéristiques, p. ex. classe, qualité)	13. Quantity (State Unit) - Quantite (Preciser l'unite)	14. Unit Price/Prix unitaire	15. Total
11	Flux	55 Gal	$1.00	$55.00
	Solder	1000 lbs	$2.50	$2,500.00

SAMPLE

18. If any of fields 1 to 17 are included on an attached commercial invoice, check this box. ☐ *Si les renseignements des zones 1 à 17 figurent sur la facure commerciale, cocher cette boite.* Commercial Invoice No. *N de facure commerciale* 12345/00	16. Total Weight (KILOS) *Poids total* Net / Gross (Brut) 680	17. Invoice Total Total de la facture $2,555.00

19. Exporter's Name and Address (If other than vendor) *Nom et adresse de l'exportateur (S'il diffère du rendeur)*	20. Originator (Name and Address) *Expéditeur d'origine (Nom et adresse)* E.X. Porter Fictitious Solder Company, Inc. 123 Park Avenue New York, NY 10001 USA

21. Departmental ruling (If applicable) *Décision du Ministère (S'il y a lieu)*	22. If fields 23 to 25 are not applicable, check this box. *Si les zones 23 à 25 sone sans objet, cocher cette boite* ☒	No. of pgs *N° de pgs* 11

23. If included in Field 17 indicate amount: *Si compris dans le total à la zone 17, préciser:* (I) Transportation charges, expenses and insurance from the place of direct shipment to Canada *Les frais de transport, dépenses et assurances à partir du point d'expédition directe vers le Canada* (II) Costs of construction, erection and assembly incurred after importation into Canada *Les coûts de contruction, d'érection et d'assemblage après importation au Canada* $_____ (III) Export packing (Le coût de l'emballage d'exportation) $_____	24. If not included in field 17 indicate amount: *Si compris dans le total à la zone 17, préciser:* (I) Transportation charges, expenses and insurance to the place of direct shipment to Canada *Les frais de transport, dépenses et assurances jusqu'au point d'expédition directe vers le Canada* $_____ (II) Amount for commissions other than buying commissions *Les commissions autres que celles versées pour l'achat* $_____ (III) Export packing (Le coût de l'emballage d'exportation) $_____	25. Check (If applicable:) *Cocher (S'il y a lieu:)* (I) Royalty payments or subsequent proceeds are paid or payable by the purchaser *Des redevances ou produits ont été ou seront versés par l'acheteur* ☐ (II) The purchaser has supplied goods or services for use in the production of these goods *L'acheteur a fourni des marchandises ou des services pour la production des marchandises* ☐

Figure 17

Department of Treasury

United States Customs Service

NORTH AMERICAN FREE TRADE AGREEMENT

19 CFR 181.11, 181.22

Certificate of Origin

1. Exporter Name and Address:	2. Blanket Period (dd/mm/yy):
Fictitious Solder Company, Inc. 123 Park Avenue New York, NY 10001	FROM: TO:

Tax Identification Number:	12-3456789

3. Producer Name and Address:	4. Importer Name and Address:
Fictitious Solder Compasny, Inc. 123 Park Avenue New York, NY 10001 USA	Canada Electronics, Inc. 123 Rue de Canada Montreal, Quebec J2L 1E3 Canada

Tax Identification Number:	12-34567890	Tax Identification Number:	

5. Description of Good(s)	6. HS Tariff Classification Number	7. Preference Criteria	8. Producer	9. Net Cost	10. Country of Origin
Flux	3810.90	B	Yes	No	US
Solder	8311.30	B	Yes	No	US

SAMPLE

I certify that:

-The information on this document is true and accurate and I assume the responsibility for proving such representations.
I understand that I am liable for any false statements or material omissions made on or in connection with this document.

-I agree to maintain, and present upon request, documentation necessary to support this certificate, and to inform,
in writing, all persons to whom the certificate was given of any changes that could affect the accuracy or validity of this certificate.

-The goods originated in the territory of one or more of the parties, and comply with the origin requirements specified for
those goods in the North American Free Trade Agreement, and unless specifically exempted in article 411 or annex 401,
there has been no further production or any other operation outside the territories of the parties; and

-The certificate consists of [1] pages, including all attachments.

11.	11a. Authorized Signature: *E X Porter*	11b. Name of Company: Fictitious Solder Company, Inc.
	11c. Name (print or type): E.X. Porter	11d. Title: Manager
	11e. Date: 00/11/19	11f. Telephone Number: (212) 555-1212 FAX: (212) 555-1313

Figure 18

CERTIFICATE OF ORIGIN

The undersigned   E.X. Porter _____   Owner

(Owner or Agent)

for Fictitious Solder Company, Inc. , 123 Park Avenue , New York, NY 10001 _____

(Name and Address of Shipper)

declares that the following mentioned goods shipped on   JAL _____

(Name of Ship)

on the date of 00/11/19   consigned to Asia Electronics KK   are products of the United States of America.

Marks and Numbers:	Number of Pkgs Boxes or Cases	Weight in Kilos		Description
		Gross	Net	
Asia Electronics KK	55	227		Flux
Asia Electronics KK	1000	454		Solder

SAMPLE

Sworn to before me

this _____ day of _____ 19 ___

Dated at ___NY___ the _18_ day of __Nov__ 2000

E.X. Porter

(Signature of Owner or Agent)

The New York Chamber of Commerce, a recognized Chamber of Commerce under the laws of the State of New York, has examined the manufacturer's invoice or shipper's affadavit concerning the origin of the merchandise and, according to the knowledge and belief, finds that the products named originated in the United States of North America.

Secretary: _____

Figure 19

Packing List

Exporter:	Intermediate Consignee:	Exporting Carrier:
Fictitious Solder Company, Inc. 123 Park Avenue New York, NY 10001		JAL
		Port/Airport of Loading:
		JFK Airport
		Foreign Port of Unloading:
		Tokyo
Ultimate Consignee:	**Forwarding Agent:**	**Date:**
Asia Electronics KK 123 Yokahama Street Tokyo Japan	Danzas AEI Cargo Building 89 Jamaica, NY 11430	00/11/19
		P.O. Number:
		987654
		Officer or Employee:
		E.X. Porter
		Type of Package:
		Skids

Carton Number:	Number of Units:	Description of Commodities:	Weight (lbs.):	Weight (Kilos):	Meas:	Marks:
1	55	Flux	500	226.8	.25 cbm	Asia Electronics KK
2 - 10	1000	Solder	1000	453.6	.75 cbm	Asia Electronics KK

SAMPLE

Our Shipment consists of | 10 | Carton(s) on | 1 | Skids

Total Pieces:	1055
Total Weight Kilos:	680.40
Total Weight LB's:	1500.00

Title: Manager   Signature: E X Porter

Figure 20

Pro Forma Invoice

Exporter:

Fictitious Solder Company, Inc.
123 Park Avenue
New York, NY 10001

Ultimate Consignee:

Asia Electronics KK
123 Yokahama Street
Tokyo
Japan

Intermediate Consignee:

Date:
00/11/19

PO Number:
987654

Customer Account Number:
5678

Pro Forma Invoice Number:
24580

Mode of Transportation:
Air

Port/Airport of Loading:
JFK Airport

Foreign Port of Unloading:
Tokyo

Ultimate Consignee Phone Number:

Pieces:	Product Name:	Product ID:	Product Description:	Harmonized Code:	Unit Price:	Total Value:
55	Flux	67890	Flux	3810.90	$1.00	$55.00
1000	Solder	12345	Solder	8311.30	$2.50	$2,500.00

SAMPLE

These commodities, technology or software were exported from the United States in accordance with the Export Administration Regulations. Diversion contrary to U.S. law prohibited.

Ex-Works Costs: $2,555.00

Other Charges:

Total:	EXW	New York		$2,555.00
				USD

Authorized Signature: E.X. Porter

Title: Manager

Figure 21

Shipper's Letter of Instruction

Fictitious Solder Company, Inc.

Forwarder: Danzas AEI Cargo Building 89 Jamaica, NY 11430	**To:** Asia Electronics KK 123 Yokahama Street Tokyo Japan	**Inland BL Number:** **Ocean BL Number:** **AWB Number:** 000-1234 5678 **Employee:** E.X. Porter **Ship VIA:** Air **Date:** 11/19/2000
From: Fictitious Solder Company, Inc. 123 Park Avenue New York, NY 10001	**Exporter's EIN #:** 12-3456789 **Exporter's Phone #:** (212) 555-1212 **Exporter's Fax #:** (212) 555-1313	**Containerized?:** ☐ Yes ☒ No **Type of Packaging:** Skids

Marks and Numbers:	Pieces:	Units:	G-Weight (lbs.):	G-Weight (Kilos):	Description of Commodities:	Schedule B:	Value:
Asia Electronics KK	55	Gal	500	226.80	Flux	3810.90.0000	$55.00
Asia Electronics KK	1000	lbs	1000	453.60	Solder	8311.30.3000	$2,500.00

SAMPLE

Inland Freight Costs: **Ocean/Air Costs:** **Handling Fees:** **Insurance Costs:** **Consular Fees:** **Additional Charges:** Quote Y/N Adjustment	☐ **YES, I would like a quote on these charges.** ☐ **YES, Please adjust invoice with these charges.** Please respond with these costs by: ○ Fax ○ Phone ○ E-Mail

Total Ex-Works: $2,555.00
Incoterm: EXW   New York

How do you want the freight billed?

○ Prepaid   ● Collect

Special Instructions

Do you require insurance?

○ Yes   ● No

License Number/Symbol:
NLR

Forward Documents To:
Buyer

Shipping Details:

● Consolidate   ○ Direct

These documents are attached to this
Shipper's Letter of Instruction:

☒ Invoice   ☒ P-List   ☐ Overland-BL
☐ NAFTA   ☒ C of O   ☐ Attachment
☒ SED   ☐ Draft

The Shipper or his Authorized Agent hereby authorizes the above named Company, in his name and on his behalf, to prepare any export documents, to sign and accept any documents relating to said shipment and forward this shipment in accordance with the conditions of carriage and the tariffs of the carriers employed. Hereunder the sole responsibility of the Company is to use reasonable care in the selection of carriers, forwarders, agents and others to whom it may entrust the shipment.

Title: Manager   **Signature:** E.X. Porter

Figure 22

specifics of someone's operation. For a more detailed treatment of this area, I recommend you source one of the many good books available concerning export documentation.

A final note, when you provide export documents to the carrier for an export shipment, make sure that you give the driver five (5) copies of each document and make sure they all are signed. This is somewhat more than you really need, but better safe than sorry. Also, be sure you retain a copy of all documents for your own records.

Schedule B

Until the late 1980s, most countries around the world used different numbering systems to classify the various commodities that are bought and sold in international trade. This caused a great deal of confusion and extra work for governments, exporters, importers and anyone else involved in international trade. Finally, under the governance of the United Nations, through the General Agreement on Tariffs and Trade (GATT), most nations agreed on a common numbering system to track goods moving in international trade. This system is known as the *Harmonized System*. The name relates to how all the participating nations are now in harmony with one another concerning this issue.

This new system provided a six digit uniform code for all commodities, and the ability for each country to add digits to the end of the initial six to provide for further levels of detail. In the United States, on the export side of the international trade coin, the Harmonized System is referred to as Schedule B, due to its location in our country's main code of export regulations. We have expanded upon the initial six digits and use a ten-digit system, with the first six corresponding to those used around the world.

When referring to this numbering system, as it applies within the United States, you can correctly call the numbers used either Schedule B numbers or harmonized numbers, as they are the same.

Governments use these numbers to track exports and to classify imports for duty calculation purposes. A representative excerpt from the tariff follows on the next page (Figure 23).

Export Controls

Within the United States, exports are controlled by several government agencies. Primary among them are the Departments of Commerce and State. Because of the pervasiveness of the Commerce Department regulations, we will focus on them. The Bureau of Export Administration (BXA) is the agency within the U.S. Department of Commerce that is responsible for developing and enforcing those Export Administration Regulations (EAR). The current regulations were enacted in 1996. They changed the BXAs approach to dealing with export controls.

Sched. B No. and Headings	Commodity Description	Unit of Quantity	Sched. B No. and Headings	Commodity Description	Unit of Quantity
3802.90	- Other:			mineral oils (including gasoline) or for other liquids used for the same purposes as mineral oils:	
3802.90.1000	- - Bone black	kg		- Antiknock preparations:	
3802.90.2000	- - Activated clays and activated earths	kg	3811.11.0000	- - Based on lead compounds	kg
3802.90.5000	- - Other	kg	3811.19.0000	- - Other	kg
3803.00.0000	Tall oil, whether or not refined	kg		- Additives for lubricating oils:	
			3811.21.0000	- - Containing petroleum oils or oils obtained from bituminous minerals	kg
3804	Residual lyes from the manufacture of wood pulp, whether or not concentrated, desugared or chemically treated, including lignin sulfonates, but excluding tall oil of heading 3803:		3811.29.0000	- - Other	kg
			3811.90.0000	- Other	kg
3804.00.1000	- Lignin sulfonic acid and its salts	kg	3812	Prepared rubber accelerators; compound plasticizers for rubber or plastics not elsewhere specified or included; antioxidizing preparations and other compound stabilizers for rubber or plastics:	
3804.00.5000	- Other	kg			
3805	Gum, wood or sulfate turpentine and other terpenic oils produced by the distillation or other treatment of coniferous woods; crude dipentene; sulfite turpentine and other crude para-cymene; pine oil containing alpha-terpineol as the main constituent:		3812.10.0000	- Prepared rubber accelerators	kg
			3812.20.0000	- Compound plasticizers for rubber or plastics	kg
			3812.30.0000	- Antioxidizing preparations and other compound stabilizers for rubber or plastics	kg
3805.10.0000	- Gum, wood or sulfate turpentine oils	liter	3813.00.0000	Preparations and charges for fire-extinguishers; charged fire-extinguishing grenades	kg
3805.20.0000	- Pine oil	kg			
3805.90.0000	- Other	kg	3814.00.0000	Organic composite solvents and thinners, not elsewhere specified or included; prepared paint or varnish removers	kg
3806	Rosin and resin acids, and derivatives thereof; rosin spirit and rosin oils; run gums:				
3806.10	- Rosin and resin acids:		3815	Reaction initiators, reaction accelerators and catalytic preparations, not elsewhere specified or included:	
3806.10.0010	- - Gum rosin	kg			
3806.10.0050	- - Other	kg		- Supported catalysts:	
3806.20.0000	- Salts of rosin or of resin acids or of derivatives of rosin or resin acids, other than salts of rosin adducts	kg	3815.11.0000	- - With nickel or nickel compounds as the active substance	kg
3806.30.0000	- Ester gums	kg	3815.12.0000	- - With precious metal or precious metal compounds as the active substance	kg
3806.90.0000	- Other	kg	3815.19.0000	- - Other	kg
			3815.90.0000	- Other	kg
3807.00.0000	Wood tar; wood tar oils; wood creosote; wood naphtha; vegetable pitch; brewers' pitch and similar preparations based on rosin, resin acids or on vegetable pitch	kg	3816	Refractory cements, mortars, concretes, and similar compositions, other than products of heading 3801:	
			3816.00.0010	- Of clay	kg
			3816.00.0050	- Other	kg
3808	Insecticides, rodenticides, fungicides, herbicides, antisprouting products and plant-growth regulators, disinfectants and similar products, put up in forms or packings for retail sale or as preparations or articles (for example, sulfur-treated bands, wicks and candles, and flypapers):		3817	Mixed alkylbenzenes and mixed alkylnaphthalenes, other than those of heading 2707 or 2902:	
			3817.10.0000	- Mixed alkylbenzenes	kg
			3817.20.0000	- Mixed alkylnaphthalenes	kg
3808.10.0000	- Insecticides	kg	3818.00.0000	Chemical elements doped for use in electronics, in the form of discs, wafers or similar forms; chemical compounds doped for use in electronics	kg
3808.20.0000	- Fungicides	kg			
3808.30.0000	- Herbicides, antisprouting products and plant-growth regulators	kg	3819.00.0000	Hydraulic brake fluids and other prepared liquids for hydraulic transmission, not containing or containing less than 70% by weight of petroleum oils or oils obtained from bituminous minerals	kg
3808.40.0000	- Disinfectants	kg			
3808.90.0000	- Other	kg			
3809	Finishing agents, dye carriers to accelerate the dyeing or fixing of dyestuffs and other products and preparations (for example, dressings and mordants), of a kind used in the textile, paper, leather or like industries, not elsewhere specified or included:		3820.00.0000	Antifreezing preparations and prepared deicing fluids	kg
			3821.00.0000	Prepared culture media for development of microorganisms	kg
3809.10.0000	- With a basis of amylaceous substances	kg	3822.00.0000	Diagnostic or laboratory reagents on a backing and prepared diagnostic or laboratory reagents whether or not on a backing, other than those of heading 3002 or 3006	kg
	- Other:				
3809.91.0000	- - Of a kind used in the textile or like industries	kg			
3809.92.0000	- - Of a kind used in the paper or like industries	kg			
3809.93.0000	- - Of a kind used in the leather or like industries	kg	3823	Industrial monocarboxylic fatty acids; acid oils from refining; industrial fatty alcohols:	
3810	Pickling preparations for metal surfaces; fluxes and other auxiliary preparations for soldering, brazing or welding; soldering, brazing or welding powders and pastes consisting of metal and other materials; preparations of a kind used as cores or coatings for welding electrodes or rods:			- Industrial monocarboxylic fatty acids; acid oils from refining:	
			3823.11.0000	- - Stearic acid	kg
			3823.12.0000	- - Oleic acid	kg
			3823.13.0000	- - Tall oil fatty acids	kg
3810.10.0000	- Pickling preparations for metal surfaces; soldering, brazing or welding powders and pastes consisting of metal and other materials	kg			
3810.90.0000	- Other	kg			
3811	Antiknock preparations, oxidation inhibitors, gum inhibitors, viscosity improvers, anticorrosive preparations and other prepared additives, for				

Figure 23

The old regulations banned all exports, then provided for specific and general licenses to allow for exportation. The current EAR specifically defines export bans and where licenses are required. Further, it provides for a number of license exceptions. Finally, it provides for the situation where neither a license nor an exception is required.

Determining the applicability of the EAR requirements for a product is a multi-step process. The first is to try and locate your item in the regulations. Where do you look? The Commerce Control List (CCL). The CCL is divided into 10 categories.

0. Nuclear Materials, Facilities and Equipment and Miscellaneous
1. Materials, Chemicals, "Microorganisms," and Toxins
2. Materials Processing
3. Electronics
4. Computers
5. Telecommunications and Information Security
6. Lasers and Sensors
7. Navigation and Avionics
8. Marine
9. Propulsion Systems, Space Vehicles and Related Equipment

Each category is further divided into five groups.

A. Equipment, Assemblies and Components
B. Test, Inspection and Production Equipment
C. Materials
D. Software
E. Technology

Items are identified in the CCL with Export Control Classification Numbers (ECCN). ECCNs are comprised of digits and letters with significance to each character position. The first character represents the general category. The second represents the group. The third signifies the reason for control. The types of reasons for control are:

0. National Security reasons
1. Missile Technology reasons
2. Nuclear Nonproliferation reasons
3. Chemical & Biological Weapons reasons
9. Anti-terrorism, Crime Control, Regional Stability, Short Supply, UN Sanctions, etc.

A typical ECCN number can look like the following. Please note the significance of the digits.

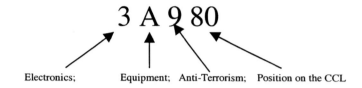

3 A 9 80

Electronics;   Equipment;   Anti-Terrorism;   Position on the CCL

After determining the appropriate ECCN, you are not quite out of the woods yet. You still must determine whether a license exception is available, check the Country Chart to see if a license is required to ship that product to the country you would like to ship to, and check the Denied Persons List to see whether it is possible to ship to that particular person or company. You can see an excerpt from the Country Chart and the Denied Persons List in figures 24 and 25.

The good news is, most items do not require a license, but you must note this on your Shipper's Export Declaration. Block 21 on the SED asks for the license required for your product. In most cases it will be the following initials, *NLR*, standing for No License Required.

The various license exceptions the bureau issues are:

- NLR – No License Required
- LVS - Limited Value Shipments.
- GBS - Group B Shipments.
- CIV - Civilian In Use.
- TSR - Technology and Software under Restriction.
- TMP - Temporary Export or Import.
- RPL - Replacements.
- GOV - Governments and International Organizations.
- GFT - Gift Parcels and Humanitarian Donations.
- AVS – Aircraft and Vessels
- BAG – Baggage
- TSU – Technology and Software Unrestricted
- APR – Additional Permissive Re-Exports
- NPR – Non-Naval Petroleum Reserves
- WRC – Western Red Cedar
- CTP - Computer

While most items do not require a license, it is important to check, just to be sure. *Do your homework!*

Supplement No. 1 to Part 738

COMMERCE COUNTRY CHART

Reason for Control / Countries	Chemical & Biological Weapons CB Column 1	CB Column 2	CB Column 3	Nuclear Nonproliferation NP Column 1	NP Column 2	National Security NS Column 1	NS Column 2	Missile Tech MT Column 1	Regional Stability RS Column 1	RS Column 2	Crime Control CC Column 1	CC Column 2	CC Column 3	Anti-Terrorism AT Column 1	AT Column 2
Japan	X					X		X	X						
Jordan	X	X	X	X		X	X	X	X	X	X		X		
Kazakhstan	X	X	X	X		X	X	X	X	X	X		X		
Kenya	X	X		X		X	X	X	X	X	X		X		
Kiribati	X	X		X		X	X	X	X	X	X		X		
Korea, North	See part 746 of the EAR to determine whether a license is required in order to export or reexport to this destination.														
Korea, South	X					X	Xe	X	X	X	X		X		
Kuwait	X	X	X	X		X	X	X	X	X	X		X		
Kyrgyzstan	X	X	X	X		X	X	X	X	X	X	X			
Laos	X	X		X		X	X	X	X	X	X	X			
Latvia	X	X		X		X	X	X	X	X	X	X			
Lebanon	X	X	X	X		X	X	X	X	X	X		X		
Lesotho	X	X		X		X	X	X	X	X	X		X		
Liberia	X	X		X		X	X	X	X	X	X		X		
Libya	See part 746 of the EAR to determine whether a license is required in order to export or reexport to this destination.														
Liechtenstein	X	X		X		X	X	X	X	X	X		X		
Lithuania	X	X		X		X	X	X	X	X	X	X			
Luxembourg	X					X		X	X						
FYROM (Macedonia)	X	X		X		X	X	X	X	X	X		X		
Madagascar	X	X		X		X	X	X	X	X	X		X		
Malawi	X	X		X		X	X	X	X	X	X		X		
Malaysia	X	X		X		X	X	X	X	X	X		X		
Maldives	X	X		X		X	X	X	X	X	X		X		
Mali	X	X		X		X	X	X	X	X	X		X		
Malta	X	X		X		X	X	X	X	X	X		X		
Marshall Islands	X	X		X		X	X	X	X	X	X		X		
Mauritania	X	X		X		X	X	X	X	X	X		X		
Mauritius	X	X		X		X	X	X	X	X	X		X		
Mexico	X	X		X		X	X	X	X	X	X		X		
Micronesia	X	X		X		X	X	X	X	X	X		X		
Moldova	X	X	X	X		X	X	X	X	X	X	X			
Monaco	X	X		X		X	X	X	X	X	X		X		
Mongolia	X	X	X	X		X	X	X	X	X	X	X			
Morocco	X	X		X		X	X	X	X	X	X		X		
Mozambique	X	X		X		X	X	X	X	X	X		X		
Namibia	X	X		X		X	X	X	X	X	X		X		
Nauru	X	X		X		X	X	X	X	X	X		X		
Nepal	X	X		X		X	X	X	X	X	X		X		
Netherlands	X					X		X	X						
New Zealand	X					X		X	X						
Nicaragua	X	X		X		X	X	X	X	X	X		X		
Niger	X	X		X		X	X	X	X	X	X		X		

Figure 24

Name and Address	Effective Date	Expiration Date	Export Privileges Affected	Federal Register Citation
d'Haens, Joseph P.M. Amerikalei 96 2000 Antwerp, Belgium and	4/25/88	4/25/08	General and validated licenses, all commodities, any destination, also exports to Canada.	53 F.R. 15582 5/2/88
Discom NV Liersesteenweg 96 2520 Ranst, Belgium and	3/13/95	4/25/08		60 F.R. 14725 3/20/95
Endymion NV Liersesteenweg 96 2520 Ranst, Belgium and	3/13/95	4/25/08		60 F.R. 14725 3/20/95
Kronatech NV Amerikalei 96 2000 Antwerp, Belgium	3/13/95	4/25/08		60 F.R. 14725 3/20/95
Diago, Michel V. 1183 Calle Del Arroy Sonoma, California	9/7/94	2/25/03	General and validated licenses, all commodities, any destination, also exports to Canada.	59 F.R. 47229 9/15/94
Didat, Jean-Michel individually and d/b/a Cotricom S.A. 4 Alles des Mesanges Yerres, France	10/8/87	Indefinite	General and validated licenses, all commodities, any destination, also exports to Canada. See: Almori, Robert	52 F.R. 38497 10/16/87
Digital Resources, Ltd. 34th Pezikow Syntagmatos 17 Pireas, Greece	2/26/86	2/26/16	General and validated licenses, all commodities, any destination, also exports to Canada. See: Simmons, Alan C.T.	51 F.R. 7476 3/4/86 51 F.R. 7481 51 F.R. 32818
Discom NV Liersesteenweg 96 2520 Ranst, Belgium	3/13/95	4/25/08	See: d'Haens, Joseph P.M.	60 F.R. 14725 3/20/95
D.J. Associates P.O. Box L Sparks, Nevada	1/31/87	1/31/07	General and validated licenses, all commodities, any destination, also exports to Canada. See: O'Hara, Daniel J.	52 F.R. 3688 2/5/87 58 F.R. 11024 2/23/95
Don Danesh	10/23/93	8/25/02	See: Danesh, Mohammad	58 F.R. 58535 11/2/93
Doornbos, GmbH Emscherstrasse 4 42697 Solingen Germany	12/18/96	12/18/00	Standard (See Korelski, Helmut)	61 F.R. 68226 12/27/96
Douglas Chua	9/10/93	9/10/13	See: Tok Peng Chua	58 F.R. 48821 9/20/93

Figure 25

One final aid: the EAR itself includes two very helpful flow charts to determine whether you are subject to the EAR and if you require an export license. They immediately follow in figures 26 and 27.

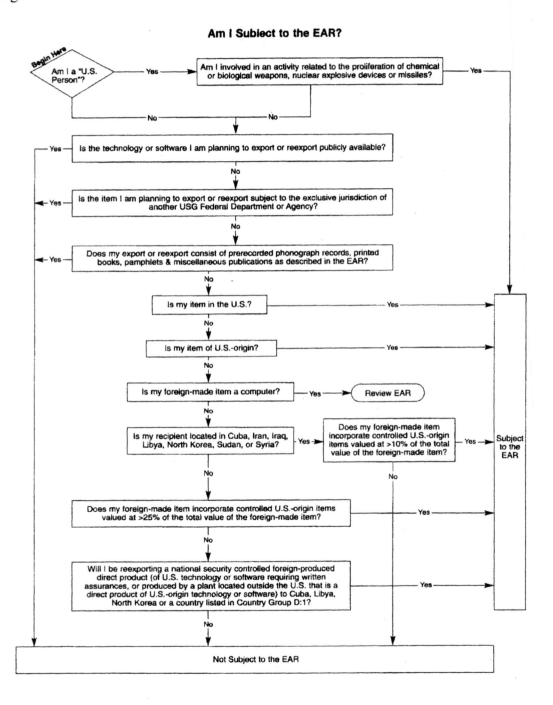

Figure 26

Decision Tree

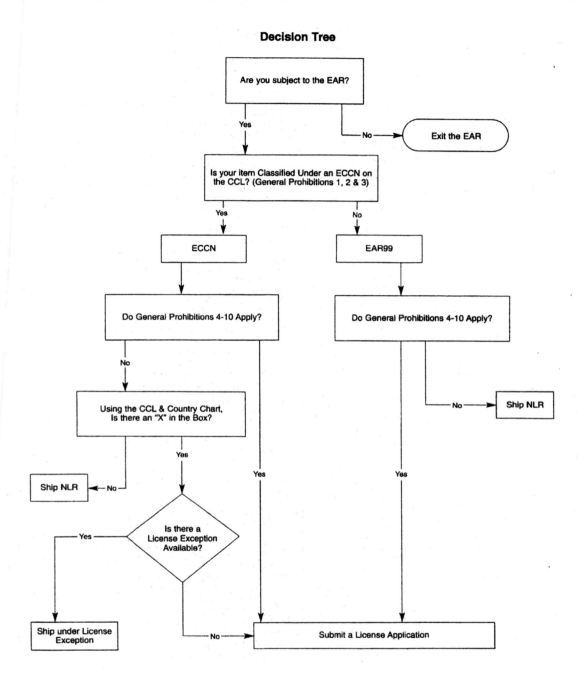

Figure 27

The Import Process

The import process is the mirror image of the export process we just finished discussing. The primary concern in having an effective import operation is meeting the documentation requirements of the U.S. Government. The critical nature of accurate, complete and proper documentation, as we discussed in the export process, really hits home in the import process. Here *you* need the correct documents or *you* cannot get your goods. Working both sides of the fence, so to speak, is a great way to appreciate the importance of good documentation. You'll find that if you run an import operation, you are more sensitive to the potential problems that can arise from incorrect or incomplete documents because you have experienced the same issues that your export customers can encounter. As such, you tend to be more aware of these issues and you find yourself doing the *right* things because you know first hand what it's like.

Documentation

The same documents are required on the import side as are required on the export side. Thanks to our discussion of exports, you are already familiar with these.

The commercial invoice is the primary document to begin the import process. Other important documents are the certificate of origin and the packing list.

Customs Brokers

All the required import documents are assembled and given to your *customs broker* for *clearance* through U.S. Customs. A customs broker is a government-licensed intermediary who acts as the importer's agent with U.S. Customs, a branch of the U.S. Department of the Treasury. Clearance refers to the process of determining the appropriate duties to be paid for a particular import shipment, paying those duties to U.S. Customs, and receiving a release from Customs so you can take possession of your merchandise.

Duties do not necessarily need to be paid prior to Customs release. Rather, an importer will post a bond with a *surety* (insurance) company, promising to pay duties in a timely manner. This is usually within 10 days of importation.

The customs broker calculates the appropriate duty rates, based upon the tariff schedule, processes the documents through U.S. Customs, obtains their release, and forwards your duty payment to Customs. They do all of this for a fee, of course. *You need a good broker!* Their services can be invaluable.

Harmonized Tariff Schedule of the United States of America (HTSUSA)

This is the tariff used to determine the applicable duty rates for the product you are importing. Remember the Harmonized and Schedule B numbers from our export discussions? Well, this is how these same numbers come into play on the import side of the operation. Your broker locates your commodity in the HTSUSA, obtains the appropriate Harmonized number, finds the applicable duty rate for that Harmonized number, and calculates the duty. Most duties are calculated on an *ad valorem* basis. That means that they are determined as a percentage of the value of the goods.

Import Duty

There are varying duty rates for the same commodity, dependent upon the country of origin (See how important that certificate of origin is?). Figure 28, shows a page from the HTSUSA. You will see that there are two columns containing different duty rates, appropriately named Column One and Column Two. Column One is further divided into general and special sub-columns. Column Two has the highest duty rates. This applies to countries of which we are not especially fond. Column One, general rates, are for those countries to which the U.S. Government has granted *Most Favored Nation* status. These apply to most countries. Column One, special rates, apply to those countries with which we have special trade agreements, such as Canada and Mexico. Recall the North American Free Trade Agreement. In many cases, for these countries, there is no duty on their products or minimal duty.

Quota

Quotas are a means of protecting domestic industries. They are a restriction on the amount of a particular commodity that may enter the United States for a specified period of time. Quotas may be based upon either the value of the goods or on the quantity of goods. They may be specific to certain countries or may be global, applying to all countries.

There is also something known as a zero-quota, prohibiting the importation of any quantity from anywhere.

Ocean Transportation

Ocean transportation is one of the oldest, still-operating modes of cargo transport. It is a reliable, cost-effective, but rather slow means of moving freight. However, if you can factor-in the transit time into your delivery requirements, it is an excellent means of moving freight in international trade.

Head/ Subhead	Stat. Suf.	Article Description	Units of Quantity	Rates of Duty		2
				1		
				General	Special	
		phenoxy]propanoate (Fenoxaprop-ethyl) and isooctyl 2,4-dichlorophenoxyacetate; Isooctyl 2-methyl-4-chloro-phenoxyacetate and application adjuvants....................				
3808.30.15	00	- - - Other	kg.............	6.5%⁴	Free (A*,CA,E,IL,J,MX)	15.4¢/kg + 31%
		- - Other:				
3808.30.20	00	- - - Containing an inorganic substance	kg.............	5%	Free (A*,CA,E,IL,J,MX)	25%
3808.30.50	00	- - - Other	kg.............	5%	Free (A+,CA,E,IL,J,MX)	25%
3808.40		- Disinfectants:				
3808.40.10	00	- - Containing any aromatic or modified aromatic disinfectant.......	kg.............	6.5%	Free (A*,CA,E,IL,J,K,MX)	15.4¢/kg + 31%
3808.40.50	00	- - Other............	kg.............	5%	Free (A*,CA,E,IL,J,K,MX)	25%
3808.90		- Other:				
		- - Containing any aromatic or modified aromatic pesticide:				
3808.90.04	00	- - - Mixtures of 1,1-bis(4-chloro- phenyl)-2,2,2-trichloroethanol (Dicofol) and application adjuvants............	kg.............	Free		15.4¢/kg + 31%
3808.90.08	00	- - - Other	kg.............	6.5%	Free (A*,CA,E,IL,J,MX)	15.4¢/kg + 31%
		- - Other:				
3808.90.30	00	- - - Formulated biocides based on 2-methyl-4-isothiazolin-3-one, or 2-n-octyl-4-isothiazolin-3-one, or 4,5-dichloro-2-n-octyl-4-isothiazolin-3-one, or mixtures of 5-chloro-2-methyl- 4-isothiazolin-3-one and 2-methyl-4-isothiazolin-3-one; and Metaldehyde............	kg.............	Free		25%
		- - - Other:				
3808.90.70	00	- - - - Containing an inorganic substance	kg.............	5%	Free (A*,CA,E,IL,J,MX)	25%
3808.90.95	00	- - - - Other	kg.............	5%	Free (A+,CA,E,IL,J) 2% (MX)	25%
3809		Finishing agents, dye carriers to accelerate the dyeing or fixing of dyestuffs and other products and preparations (for example, dressings and mordants), of a kind used in the textile, paper, leather or like industries, not elsewhere specified or included:				
3809.10.00	00	- With a basis of amylaceous substances	kg.............	2.6¢/kg + 3.5%	Free (A*,CA,E,IL,J,MX)	17.6¢/kg + 25%
		- Other:				
3809.91.00	00	- - Of a kind used in the textile or like industries	kg.............	6%	Free (A*,CA,E,IL,J,MX)	25%
3809.92		- - Of a kind used in the paper or like industries:				
3809.92.10	00	- - - Containing 5% or more by weight of one or more aromatic or modified aromatic substances............	kg.............	9.2%	Free (A+,CA,E,IL,J,MX)	60%
3809.92.50	00	- - - Other	kg.............	6%	Free (A+,CA,E,IL,J,MX)	25%
3809.93		- - Of a kind used in the leather or like industries:				
3809.93.10	00	- - - Containing 5% or more by weight of one or more aromatic or modified aromatic substances............	kg.............	9.2%	Free (A+,CA,E,IL,J) 4.8% (MX)	60%
3809.93.50	00	- - - Other	kg.............	6%	Free (A+,CA,E,IL,J) 2.4% (MX)	25%
3810		Pickling preparations for metal surfaces; fluxes and other auxiliary preparations for soldering, brazing or welding; soldering, brazing or welding powders and pastes consisting of metal and other materials; preparations of a kind used as cores or coatings for welding electrodes or rods:				
3810.10.00	00	- Pickling preparations for metal surfaces; soldering, brazing or welding powders and pastes consisting of metal and other materials............	kg.............	5%	Free (A+,CA,E,IL,J) 2% (MX)	25%
3810.90		- Other:				
3810.90.10	00	- - Containing 5% or more by weight of one or more aromatic or modified aromatic substances............	kg.............	1.8¢/kg + 10%	Free (A+,CA,E,IL,J,MX)	3.7¢/kg + 60%
3810.90.20	00	- - Consisting wholly of inorganic substances............	kg.............	Free		25%
3810.90.50	00	- - Other	kg.............	5%	Free (A+,CA,E,IL,J,MX)	25%
3811		Antiknock preparations, oxidation inhibitors, gum inhibitors, viscosity improvers, anticorrosive preparations and other prepared additives, for mineral oils (including gasoline) or for other liquids used for the same purposes as mineral oils: - Antiknock preparations:				
3811.11		- - Based on lead compounds:				
3811.11.10	00	- - - Based on tetraethyl lead or on a mixture of tetraethyl lead and tetramethyl lead............	kg.............	Free		30%
3811.11.50	00	- - - Other	kg.............	Free		25%

Figure 28

Typical transit time from the U.S. west coast to the pacific rim is about 11 days. The transit time form the U.S. east coast to Europe is approximately nine to 10 days.

As you would suspect, the primary document in ocean transport is the ocean bill of lading. In purpose and most detail, is similar to a motor freight bill of lading. It is important to recognize that an ocean bill of lading may or may not be a negotiable instrument. In other words, physical possession of the original document may be required to take possession of the goods covered by the bill of lading. The simplest way to determine whether it is negotiable or not is to look at the wording in the consignee block. If the shipment is consigned "to the order of the shipper", then the consignee must surrender the original B/L to the carrier to take possession of the cargo. If it consigned directly to the consignee, then the original document is not required. Generally, you decide how to consign the bill of lading based upon credit issues associated with the consignee. I have provided an example ocean B/L in figure 29.

Ocean Carriers

Ocean freight carriers are those companies that actually own and operate the huge ocean-going vessels. There are three primary types of cargo vessels:

- Container Ships - The freight is stowed in either 20' or 40' weather-tight ocean containers.
- Bulk Carriers - The most common here is the tanker - moving crude oil, etc.
- Ro-Ro Vessels - Roll-On/Roll-Off ships where motorized cargo, such as automobiles, construction machinery or trucks are actually driven on and off of the ships.

Most shippers will make use of containerized freight. This freight is sold either in full-container loads *(FCL)* or Less-Than-Container loads *(LCL)*. As in the case of motor freight, full loads cost less per pound or kilogram than partially full loads.

Non-Vessel Operating Common Carriers (NVOCC)

NVOCCs, or NVOs for short, consolidate small shipments from multiple shippers into full container loads. They arrange for all details of the transportation move with the ocean carrier. They make their money by the difference between the full container rate they pay the steamship line, over the LCL rate they charge the shipper.

Freight Forwarders

Forwarders have large-scale relationships with both ocean freight and air freight carriers. Because of their substantial buying power, they can offer considerable cost savings to the shipper. They also assist in choosing the right carrier for the move, preparing

Ocean Bill of Lading

Exporter (Name and address including ZIP code) Fictitious Solder Company, Inc. 123 Park Avenue New York, NY 10001	Document Number	Booking Number QOCS-1234/01
	Export References	

Consigned To Asia Electronics KK 123 Yokohama Street Tokyo Japan	Forwarding Agent (Name and address) Danzas AEI Cargo Building 89 Jamaica, NY 11430

Notify Party	Point (State) of Origin or FTZ Number New York
	Domestic Routing/Export Instructions

Pre-Carriage By Jamaica Cartage	Place of Receipt By Pre-Carrier Tokyo	
Exporting Carrier Quick Ocean Carrier	Port of Loading/Export JFK Airport	
Foreign Port of Unloading Tokyo	Place of Delivery By On-Carrier Tokyo	Type of Move Vessel

Marks and Numbers	Number of Packages	Description of Commodities in Schedule B Detail	Gross Weight (Kilos)	Measurement
Asia Electronics KK	55	Flux	227	.25 cbm
Asia Electronics KK	1000	Solder	454	.75 cbm

SAMPLE

There are 1 pages, including attachments to this Ocean Bill of Lading

These commodities, technology or software were exported from the United States in accordance with the Export Administration Regulations. Diversion contrary to U.S. law prohibited.

Carrier has a policy against payment solicitation, or receipt of any rebate, directly or indirectly, which would be unlawful under the United States Shipping Act, 1984 as amended.

FREIGHT RATES, CHARGES, WEIGHTS AND/OR MEASUREMENTS

SUBJECT TO CORRECTION	PREPAID	COLLECT
Ocean Freight Minimum		$200.00
THC		$25.00
Bunker Surcharge		$10.00
CAF		$50.00
GRAND TOTAL	$0.00	$285.00

Received by Carrier for shipment by ocean vessel between port of loading and port of discharge, and for arrangement or procurement of pre-carriage from place of receipt and on-carriage to place of delivery, where stated above, the goods as specified above in apparent good order and condition unless otherwise stated. The goods to be delivered at the above mentioned port of discharge or place of delivery, whichever is applicable.

IN WITNESS WHEREOF 3 original Bills of Lading have been signed, not otherwise stated above, one of which being accomplished the others shall be void.

DATED AT _____

BY _____

Agent for the Carrier

Mo.	Day	Year

B/L No.
QOCS-1234/01

Figure 29

documentation and notifying the consignee about the arrival of their shipment. They may also serve as Customs Brokers and/or NVOCCs.

Rates & Pricing

Full container loads are quoted on a price per container basis. The forwarder will quote you a flat fee covering the move from port-to-port.

LCL shipments are priced, based upon the weight or measurement (**W/M**) of the shipment; whichever produces the greater revenue for the carrier. The pricing is quoted in dollars per 2,200# or 1,0000 kilograms (weight), or 40 cubic feet or one cubic meter (measurement). On this basis, the quote you will receive will be stated as, for example: $50 weight or measure *(W/M)*. So, you multiply the price by the weight or measurement factor, and whichever one is higher will be the price you pay.

There can also be some accessorial charges involved as well here. At certain times, you may be charged what is called a ***Bunker Surcharge***, which is another name for a fuel surcharge. This is applied in times when the cost of fuel is high. Also, you may be assessed a ***Currency Adjustment Factor*** (CAF). This is done at times when the value of the U.S. dollar is low, relative to other currencies. A ***Terminal Handling Charge*** will typically be assessed as well. This charge covers the movement of the freight while it is on the pier.

Air Transportation

Air transportation, on an international basis, is very similar to domestic air transport. The players are largely the same, except that you now also deal with carriers from foreign nations as well.

As in the case of domestic air transport, the central document is the air waybill. Figure 30 displays an international air waybill.

Air Carriers

The all-cargo airlines and the passenger airlines are both big players in international airfreight. In general, your main point of contact for international airfreight will be an international freight forwarder, as they can provide the most competitive pricing, thanks to their volume commitments to the various airlines.

House Air Waybill Number
JFK 123456

Shipper's Name and Address:

Fictitious Solder Company, Inc.
123 Park Avenue
New York, NY 10001

Shipper's account Number
123456

Not negotiable

Air Waybill
(Air Consignment note)
Issued by

Best Forwarding, Inc.
123 Main Street
Chicago, IL 60001

Copies 1, 2 and 3 of this Air Waybill are originals and have the same validity

Consignee's Name and Address:

Asia Electronics KK
123 Yokahama Street
Tokyo

Japan

Consignee's account Number
654321

It is agreed that the good described herein are accepted in apparent good order and condition (except as noted) for carriage AUBJECT TO THE CONDITIONS OF CONTRACT ON THE REVERSE HEREOF, THE SHIPPER'S ATTENTION IS DRAWN TO THE NOTICE CONCERNING CARRIERS' LIMITATION OF LIABILITY. Shipper may increase such limitation of liability by declaring a higher value for carriage and paying a supplemental charge if required.

These commodities, technology or software were exported from the United States in accordance with the Export Administration Regulations. Diversion contrary to U.S. law prohibited.

Airport of Departure (Addr. of first Carrier) and requested Routing
JFK Airport, New York

to	By first Carrier	Routing and Destination	Air Waybill Number	Currency	CHGS Code	WT/VAL		Other		Declared Value for Carriage	Declared Value for Customs
						PPD	COLL	PPD	COLL		
TYO			000-1234 5678	USD		X		X		NVD	NVD

Airport of Destination	Flight/Date	For Carrier Use only Flight/Date	Amount of Insurance	INSURANCE: If Carrier offers insurance and such insurance is requested in accordance with conditions on revers hereof, indicate amount to be insured in figures in box marked "amount
Tokyo	BF123/11			

Handling Information
Do not double stack!

No. of Pieces RCP	Gross Weight	kg lb	Rate Class / Commodity Item No.	Chargeable Weight	Rate / Charge	Total	Nature and Quantity of Goods (incl. Dimensions or Volume)
1	226.8	K		226.8	2.20	498.96	Tin/Lead Solders
							Origin: USA
							Freight: Prepaid
							Inv. No. FS98765/00

SAMPLE

Prepaid	Weight Charge	**Collect**	Other Charges
498.96			FSC 22.68 TSF 30.00
	Valuation Charge		
	Tax		
	Total other Charges Due Agent		Shipper certifies that the particulars on the face hereof are correct and that insofar as any part of the consignment contains dangerous goods, such part is properly described by name and is in proper condition for carriage by air according to the applicable Dangerous Goods Regulations.
52.68			
	Total other Charges Due Carrier		

Signature of Shipper or his Agent

Total prepaid		Total collect	
551.64			08.DEC.2000 JFK
Currency Conversion Rates	cc charges in Dest. Currency		Executed on (Date) at (Place) Signature of Issuing Carrier or its Agent

House Air Waybill Number
JFK 123456

Figure 30

Freight Forwarders

As mentioned above, these are the folks you want to deal with for international airfreight. There are many old, established firms in this arena, as well as some newer major players. The forwarder prepares the air waybill, based upon the information provided by you through a Shipper's Letter of Instruction and your other export documents. They may also prepare the Shipper's Export Declaration for you.

Pricing is quoted on a cost per kilogram basis, with the rate per kilo declining as the weight increases. The forwarder can give you a price for a number of different levels of service. They can offer you pricing on a door-to-door basis, door-to-airport basis or airport-to-airport basis. They will also offer different pricing if you want the next available flight to destination, which is sometimes called an *IATA* (International Air Transport Association) move. This is the full price that an airline would charge you for their service. Or, more typically, you would want their *consolidation* pricing. This is where the forwarder assembles the freight from a number of shippers over the course of a few days and then consolidates them to maximize the cost savings. Most forwarders offer a consolidation *(consol)* two or three times per week to most airports around the world.

In the case of a consolidation, two air waybills are issued: a *master air waybill* and a *house air waybill*. The master air waybill is the air waybill covering all of the freight in the consolidation. It issued by the airline. The house air waybill is that which covers your freight in particular. The forwarder issues this. In tracking your freight, you need to know both of these air waybill numbers and the forwarder will provide you with them.

Your pricing will be offered in dollars per kilogram (2.2046 pounds). A sample rate chart follows:

Origin:	Newark, NJ					
Destination:	Paris	Minimum	<100K	>100K	>300K
		$60.00	$2.00	$1.80	$1.70

Some of the more well known international freight forwarders are:

- Danzas AEI
- BAX Global
- Schenker International
- Expediters International
- Kuehne & Nagel

International Terms of Sale (Incoterms)

Incoterms are the international equivalent of the domestic terms of sale we covered earlier. Does anyone remember FOB? I hope so.

Incoterms stands for international commercial terms. The chosen Incoterm is a term of the contract of sale. Their purpose is to:

- Standardize the trade terms used in international contracts of sale
- Develop the rules of interpretation for these terms
- Explain the division of costs and risks between the various parties to an international sale

Incoterms are developed and published by the International Chamber of Commerce. The first edition was published way back in 1936. They are revised every ten years or so, with the preceding revision dating back to 1990. The current version was released in 2000 to improve consistency in the application of the terms and update the preceding revision to reflect current commercial practice.

There are 13 different trade terms, classified into four groups, with each group beginning with the same letter designation - E, F, C and D. The following table explains the assignment of the rights, risks and responsibilities associated with each term (Figure 31).

As you read the table on the next couple of pages, you may see some unfamiliar terminology. I'd like to clear it up for you right now.

In the Incoterm DEQ - Delivered Ex Quay, the word 'quay' means wharf or pier. It is pronounced 'key'.

Pre-carriage is inland freight at the origin of the goods – in other words, the freight from the factory to the port.

Main carriage is the freight from port to port or the line haul.

On-carriage is the inland freight at the destination – in other words, the freight from the port to the customer.

Group	Incoterm	Mode of Transportation	Seller's Responsibility	Buyer's responsibility	Passage of Risk
E Group	EXW – Ex Works	Determined by buyer (all modes)	• Goods • Export Packing	• Pre-Carriage • Export Clearance • Main Carriage • Import Clearance • On-Carriage	When goods are made available by seller at named location.
F Group	FCA – Free Carrier (named place)	All modes	• Goods • Export Packing • Loading on vehicle • Pre-Carriage • Export Clearance	• Main Carriage • Import Clearance • On-Carriage	When goods are delivered to carrier at named place.
	FAS – Free Alongside Ship (named port of shipment)	Ocean only	• Goods • Export Packing • Pre-carriage • Export Clearance	• Vessel Loading • Main Carriage • Import Clearance • On-Carriage	When goods are delivered alongside ship specified by buyer.
	FOB – Free on Board (named port of shipment)	Ocean only	• Goods • Export Packing • Pre-Carriage • Export Clearance • Vessel Loading	• Main Carriage • Import Clearance • On-Carriage	When goods cross the ship's rail at port of shipment.
C Group	CFR – Cost and Freight (named port of destination)	Ocean only	• Goods • Export Packing • Pre-Carriage • Export Clearance • Vessel Loading • Main Carriage Payment	• Goods in Main Carriage Transit • Import Clearance • On-Carriage	When goods cross the ship's rail at port of shipment. Buyer secures own insurance.
	CIF – Cost, Insurance and Freight (named port of destination)	Ocean only	• The same as CFR plus ocean cargo insurance	• The same as CFR	When goods cross the ship's rail at port of shipment. If loss or damage, buyer files claim.
	CPT – Carriage Paid To (named place of destination)	All modes	• Goods • Export Packing • Export Clearance • Delivery to First Carrier • Main Carriage Payment	• Goods in Carrier Custody • Goods in Main Carriage Transit • Import Clearance • On-Carriage	When goods are delivered by the seller to the first carrier. Buyer secures own insurance

Figure 31

Group	Incoterm	Mode of Transportation	Seller's Responsibility	Buyer's responsibility	Passage of Risk
	CIP – Carriage and Insurance Paid To (named place of destination)	All modes	• Same as CPT plus ocean cargo insurance	• The same as CPT	When goods are delivered by the seller to the first carrier. If loss or damage, buyer files claim.
D Group	**DAF** – Delivered at Frontier (named place)	Typically rail, can be for all modes	• Goods • Export Packing • Pre-carriage to border • Export Clearance	• Import Clearance • On-Carriage from Border	When the goods are handed over to the buyer at the named frontier point.
	DES – Delivered Ex Ship (named port of destination)	Ocean only	• Goods • Export Packing • Pre-carriage • Export Clearance • Vessel Loading • Main Carriage to Named Port	• Vessel Unloading • Import Clearance • On-Carriage	When the goods are ready for unloading by the buyer at port of destination.
	DEQ – Delivered Ex Quay (named port of destination)	Ocean only	• Goods • Export Packing • Pre-Carriage • Export Clearance • Vessel Loading/Unloading • Main Carriage	• On-Carriage • Import Clearance	When the goods are placed on the dock or in a terminal.
	DDU – Delivered Duty Unpaid (named place of destination)	All modes	• Goods • Export Packing • Pre-Carriage • Export Clearance • Main Carriage • On-Carriage	• Import Clearance	When goods are delivered at location specified. Seller should insure goods.
	DDP – Delivered Duty Paid (named place of destination)	All modes	• Everything associated with the shipment	• Take delivery of goods at buyer's premises	When goods are delivered to buyer at specified location. Seller should insure goods.

Figure 31 cont'd.

While the preceding table is nice as a means of listing many of the specifics of the various Incoterms; to the uninitiated, it probably doesn't mean a great deal. I have found that to get a better sense for where each Incoterm applies, the following illustration is particularly helpful (Figure 32). The best way to read this illustration is from left to right. As you move further to the right, the level of risk and responsibility increases for the seller. EXW results in the lowest level of risk to the seller, while DDP yields the highest level of risk and responsibility for the seller.

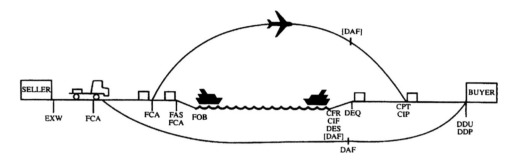

NOTES

1. On CFR, CIF, CPT, and CIP shipments delivery and risk of loss transfer to buyer at port of *shipment*, although seller is responsible for paying for costs of freight (CFR, CPT) and insurance (CIF, CIP).

2. Except for CIP and CIF sales (where insurance is part of the contract price), the seller is not required to purchase insurance but may do so up to the place of delivery, which becomes a cost to be factored into the seller's profitability and sales quotation.

3. Under CIF and CIP, seller must only provide minimum coverage (110% of contract price) but no war risk or strike, riot, and civil commotion coverage unless buyer agrees to bear expense.

4. Packing costs for shipment to known ultimate destination are an expense of the seller (even on EXW sales).

5. Cost of pre-shipment inspections are always the expense of the buyer unless inspections are required by country of exportation or otherwise agreed in the sales contract.

By viewing this illustration in conjunction with the tables, the various Incoterms should be much more comprehensible. By the way, the illustration and associated notes are from an excellent book by Thomas E. Johnson called *Export/Import Procedures and Documentation*. It is by far the most comprehensive treatment I have ever seen of the export/import process and it is highly recommended. Everyone in the field should have a copy on their personal bookshelf.

International Sales Transactions

Sales transactions in an international environment are much more complicated and risk prone than your typical sale within the United States. If you have a problem collecting your payment from a foreign customer, it is very difficult and expensive to bring a law suit against that customer because the laws of the United States may not apply.

There are ways however, to minimize this risk exposure. We will look at some of these in the discussion that follows and also talk about the risk-heavy, but familiar method that we normally use in domestic transactions.

Letter of Credit

A letter of credit, normally referred to as an *L/C*, is the most common method of reducing payment risk in international sales transactions. A letter of credit can be defined as "a conditional undertaking by a bank, issued in accordance with the instructions of the *account party*, addressed to or in favor of the *beneficiary*. The bank promises to pay, accept, or negotiate the beneficiary's *draft* up to a certain sum of money, in the stated currency, within the prescribed time limit, upon the presentation of stipulated documents." (Schaffer, Earle & Agusti, p. 263) Whew! What a mouthful. Now let's translate this.

A letter of credit is a means for a shipper to collect payment for his goods from the customer. It involves a formal document, with specific terms and conditions, which requires the shipper to deliver the correct product within a certain period of time, to the customer. It then obliges the customer to make funds available to the shipper for payment, before the freight can be obtained.

The transaction involves two banks - the customer's and the shipper's. The customer is known as the account party or *applicant*. The shipper is known as the *beneficiary*.

The customer opens a letter of credit with his bank. This document states, in very explicit terms, exactly what the customer wants and when he wants it. The customer must set aside the funds with his bank to pay for this shipment.

The shipper, if he accepts the terms of the letter of credit, must meet those terms before he can be paid for his goods. The official letter of credit document is forwarded by the customer's bank to the shipper (beneficiary). When the shipper is ready to ship his freight to the customer, he submits all of the documents required by the letter of credit, along with a copy of the credit, and a draft for payment, to either his bank or a local branch of the customer's bank. The draft is the demand for payment.

The bank forwards these documents to the customer's local bank; he and the customer review completeness of the documents and whether the other terms of the L/C are met, and if all is well, the customer's bank forwards the funds for payment, back through the various banks to the shipper.

Any errors in the execution of the L/C are called *discrepancies*. For the shipper to be paid, all discrepancies must either be fixed or *waived* (disregarded). This whole process can be quite bureaucratic and time consuming.

Even the slightest deviation from the terms of the L/C will generate a discrepancy. You must follow the terms of the L/C to the letter, or you will be in for a paperwork nightmare.

While it sounds complicated, and it is, it does virtually guarantee payment from the customer, *as long as the shipper does things right!*

The most common types of drafts are *sight drafts* and *time drafts*. Sight drafts are a demand for payment upon the presentation, in good order, of the required documents. When the documents are approved, the funds are released to the shipper. A time draft works the same, except the payment is released after a specified amount of time, e.g. 30 days, 60 days, etc. These terms are spelled out in the letter of credit.

An example of a letter of credit and a draft are submitted in figures 33 and 34.

Open Account

This is the usual method for selling goods within the United States. A company ships their product to their customer, they mail them a bill, and within 30 days or so, the customer mails back a check for payment in full. Clean and simple!

Well, I don't recommend this method in most cases when selling internationally. In that market, you do not have the long arm of Uncle Sam on your side. So, if you don't get paid, you are now dealing with a completely different government, with different laws and regulations. Good luck trying to collect if there is a problem!

This method is usually used when shipping to your own subsidiary overseas. Then you have control over your own people. I really wouldn't recommend this method under any other conditions unless you *really* know your customer. *Be forewarned!*

Bill of Exchange (Direct Collection)

A bill of exchange (direct collection) transaction works mechanically the same as a letter of credit transaction. The documents are forwarded through the banking channels and payment is forwarded back through the same banks. The difference is that there is no letter of credit.

This is used where there may be currency restrictions within a country. The government tries to restrict the outflow of dollars from their country. In such a case, the government will not allow the funds to be released without complete documentation of the transaction. This type of transaction occurs in trade with India and some other countries. At its simplest level, this type of transaction is a draft and document submission without the letter of credit.

OUR ADVICE NUMBER HNYE-72682
FROM : HANIL BANK SEOUL KOREA, REPUBLIC OF

SEPTEMBER 23 1997

To: ALPHA METALS INC.
    600 ROUTE 440   JERSEY
    CITY, NJ   07304
    USA

OUR ADVICE
No. HNYE-72682
HANIL BANK
NEW YORK AGENCY
399 PARK AVENUE
NEW YORK, N.Y. 10022

AUTHORIZED SIGNATURE

MType:700 Issue of a Documentary Credit

40A	FORM OF DC	: IRREVOCABLE
20	DC NO	: M1940709NU00527
31C	DATE OF ISSUE	: 22SEP97
31D	EXPIRY DATE AND PLACE	: 21DEC97 BENEFICIARY IN YOUR COUNTRY
50	APPLICANT	: HYUNDAI CORP, SEOUL, KOREA.
59	BENEFICIARY	: ALPHA METALS INC.
		600 ROUTE 440 JERSEY
		CITY, NJ 07304
		USA
32B	DC AMOUNT	: USD21,500.00
39B	MAXIMUM CREDIT AMOUNT	: MAXIMUM
41	AVAILABLE WITH	: ANY BANK
	AVAILABLE BY	BY NEGOTIATION
42C	DRAFTS AT...	: 90DAYS AFTER B/L DATE(NU)
42	DRAWEE	: HANIHKHH
		HANIL BANK. HONG KONG BRANCH
		BANK OF AMERICA TOWER
		FLOOR 13
		HONG KONG
43P	PARTIAL SHIPMENT	: ALLOWED
43T	TRANSSHIPMENT	: PROHIBITED
44A	SHIPMENT FROM:	
	USA AIRPORT	
44B	FOR TRANSPORTATION TO:	
	KIMPO AIRPORT	
44C	LATEST DATE OF SHIPMENT	: 21NOV97
71B	CHARGES	: ALL BANKING CHARGES INCLUDING
		REIMBURSEMENT CLAIM CHARGE OUTSIDE
		KOREA ARE FOR ACCOUNT OF THE
		BENEFICIARY
48	PERIOD FOR PRESENTATION	: TRANSPORT DOCUMENTS MUST BE
		PRESENTED WITHIN 07 DAYS AFTER
		THE DATE OF SHIPMENT BUT WITHIN

Figure 33

OUR ADVICE NUMBER HNYE-72682   PAGE NO: 2
FROM : HANIL BANK SEOUL KOREA, REPUBLIC OF

                                THE EXPIRY DATE OF THIS CREDIT.   ┌─────────────────────┐
  49   CONFIRMATION INSTRUCTIONS: WITHOUT   │ OUR ADVICE   │
  53   REIMBURSEMENT BANK   : HANIHKHH   │ No. *MNYE-72682*   │
                                   HANIL BANK, HONG KONG BRANCH   │ HANIL BANK   │
                                   BANK OF AMERICA TOWER   │ NEW YORK AGENCY   │
                                   FLOOR 13   │ 399 PARK AVENUE   │
                                   HONG KONG   │ NEW YORK, N.Y. 10022│
  78   INSTRUCTION TO PAY: │   │
       TO PAY /ACC/NEG/ BK :   │ AUTHORIZED SIGNATURE│
       THE AMOUNT OF EACH DRAFT MUST BE ENDORSED   └─────────────────────┘
       ON THE REVERSE OF THIS CREDIT
       +ALL DOCUMENTS MUST BE FORWARDED TO US BY
       COURIER SERVICE IN ONE LOT. ADDRESSED TO HANIL BANK
           130, NAMDAEMUNRO 2-GA, CHUNG GU, SEOUL KOREA
        +BENEFICIARY'S USANCE DRAFTS MUST BE NEGOTIATED AT SIGHT BASIS
       AND PRESENTED TO DRAWEE BANK FOR DISCOUNT AT BUYER'S ACCOUNT
       +REIMBURSEMENTS IS SUBJECT TO ICC URR525.
  45   COVERING:
       TERMS OF PRICE   FOB
       USA AIRPORT
       COUNTRY OF ORIGIN   UNITED STATES
       RINSE EFFECTIVENESS TEST 1SET
       HEI P.O NO ACO70703FBF9708051 (BAF-7-0140) USD21500.00
       APPEND OF ORIGIN
  46   DOCUMENTS REQUIRED:
       SIGNED COMMERCIAL INVOICE IN 03 COPIES
       AIRWAY BILL CONSIGNED TO HANIL BANK
       MARKED FREIGHT COLLECT AND
       NOTIFY HYUNDAI ELECTRONICS IND CO., LTD.
       PACKING LIST IN 03 COPIES
  47   ADDITIONAL CONDITIONS:
       Other additional conditions
       HAWB ISSUED BY NEW WORLD FREIGHT SYSTEM ONLY SHALL BE ACCEPTABLE.
       WHEN NEGOTIATING BANK CLAIM REIMBURSEMENT, THEY SHOULD INDICATE
       THE DATE OF BILL OF LADING (OR AIR WAY BILL) ON THE LETTER OF REI
       MBURSEMENT CLAIM.
       IF DOCUMENTS CONTAINING DISCREPANCIES ARE PRESENTED,
       A FEE OF USD40 (OR EQUIVALENT) SHOULD BE DEDUCTED FROM
       THE REIMBURSEMENT CLAIM. NOTWITHSTANDING ANY
       INSTRUCTION TO THE CONTRARY,
       THIS FEE SHOULD BE CHARGED TO THE BENEFICIARY.

  YOURS VERY TRULY,   ADVISING BANK'S NOTIFICATION

  AUTHORIZED SIGNATURE   PLACE, DATE, NAME AND SIGNATURE
                                       OF ADVISING BANK

Figure 33 cont'd.

Ref. No. **ABC12345**   Place: **New York, NY 10001 USA**   Date: **Nov. 26, 2000**

At _____ **Sight**

Pay to the order of **Fictitious Solder Company, Inc.**   U.S.$ 20,000.00

Twenty Thousand and no/100   **US Dollars**

Drawee First National Bank of Japan
P.O. Box 12345
Tokyo, Japan

Drawer Fictitious Solder Company, Inc.
123 Park Avenue
New York, NY 10001

Drawn under documentary credit number A123456789
dated September 1, 2000.

E.X. Porter

Authorized Signature

- -

Date: Nov. 26, 2000   Reference Number: ABC12345

Sir/Madam: We enclose the following for collection. Please handle this collection in accordance with the Uniform Rules for Collections in effect at the time of this transaction, currently ICC Publication URC 522.

Documents	Comm. Inv.	Cust. Inv.	Neg. B/L	NoNeg B/L	Air Way Bill	Insur. Cert.	Certif. Origin	Draft	Pkg. List	Miscellaneous
O / C	5		3	2		2	4	1	5	

Fate & Proceeds:

Advise Payment/Acceptance by:

○ Airmail   ○ Telex   ● SWIFT

☐ Advise dishonor by cable giving reasons.

Charges:

Collection charges for:

● Our Account   ○ Their Account

☐ All charges are payable by drawee—waive if refused.
☐ All charges are payable by drawee—do not waive.
☐ A provisional deposit in local currency may be accepted.

When Paid:

☒ CREDIT our ACCOUNT NO 987654321
☐ Send PAYMENT to us by check, to the address below.

Documents:

☒ Deliver documents against payment if sight draft.
☐ Deliver documents against acceptance if time draft.
☐ Documents to be mailed in two mails.
☐ Collecting bank may delay presentation until arrival of vessel carying goods.

Protest:

Protest Non-Payment/Non-Acceptance. Advise us by:

○ Airmail   ○ Telex   ● SWIFT

☐ Do not protest.

Interest:

Collect interest at   % per annum
from   to

In case of need, refer to:
E.X. Porter
Fictitous Solder Company, Inc.
123 Park Avenue New York, NY 10001 USA 212-555-1212

☐ Who has no authority to change these instructions.
☒ Whose instructions may be followed in every respect.
☐ Whose instructions may be followed except as noted below.

Special Instructions:

E.X. Porter

Authorized Signature

Figure 34

Free Trade Agreements

Free trade agreements are treaties between governments designed to break down the barriers to trade between the participating countries. These barriers can include restrictions on the type and quantity of products traded or customs duties, which make imported products more expensive. There are a number of agreements of this type in effect around the world. We will talk about the one that you will be most likely to encounter - the North American Free Trade Agreement (NAFTA).

North American Free Trade Agreement

If you do business within North America, then the North American Free Trade Agreement will affect you. We discussed this earlier during our look at export documentation. NAFTA became effective on January 1, 1994. Its purpose is to reduce and ultimately eliminate duties on products manufactured in, and traded between, the United States, Canada and Mexico. By the way, Canada and Mexico are the United States' two largest trading partners.

The ultimate goal of the trade agreement is to have totally free trade in NAFTA eligible goods among all three parties to the treaty. Those three parties are Canada, Mexico and the U.S. It was decided that the entire phase out program should take 15 years, so the scheduled completion date was 2008.

The important point here is to realize that the preferential duty treatment applies only on those goods made in one of the three NAFTA countries. Therefore, when you prepare a NAFTA Certificate of Origin, you are declaring that the goods you are shipping are made in the U.S., Canada or Mexico.

Negotiating International Freight Pricing

Negotiating international freight pricing is very similar to domestic pricing negotiations. The more information you can give the forwarder/carrier, the better. They will want to know your origins, destinations, commodities, volume per lane, mode of shipment (air/ocean), specialized handling characteristics (hazardous, refrigeration required, etc.), transit time expectations and any other pertinent details you can provide.

If you have a significant amount of international freight, you may want to take a formal approach to negotiations with the participating forwarders. To do this, you submit to each participant a detailed presentation of your freight volumes and service expectations. This document is generally referred to as a request for proposal (RFP) or a request for quotation (RFQ).

By using this method, you are sure that all the participants are bidding from the same set of information. This ensures that when you assess their capabilities, you are comparing apples to apples, so to speak.

Appendix E contains a sample RFP that I have used successfully. Feel free to use it as a model for yourself. If you are really diligent, you can take this format and modify it for use in your domestic freight negotiations as well. Good luck!

Chapter 3

Warehousing

Introduction

According to Kenneth Ackerman's exhaustive 1986 work, *Practical Handbook of Warehousing*, warehousing is the storage of commodities and products for profit. Our concern in this chapter will be the function of the private warehouse. A private warehouse is one owned and operated by a company for its own personal use.

Ackerman maintains that there are six major functions of warehousing. These are:

- Stockpiling
- Product mixing
- Production logistics
- Consolidation
- Distribution
- Customer service

Stockpiling makes use of the warehouse's storage capabilities to accommodate production overflow. **Product mixing** allows a company with multiple diverse product lines to consolidate their diverse products at one central warehouse location for later distribution. **Production logistics** entails storing semi-finished goods for limited periods of time to eventually fulfill production needs in a factory on a just-in-time (JIT) basis. **Consolidation** involves using a warehouse as a gathering point for product to assemble them for later shipment to their eventual destination. **Distribution**, the opposite of consolidation, is the process of shipping finished goods to the market place. Warehouses provide **customer service** by offering a manufacturer's local presence to various markets.

General Warehouse Operations

As a result of vastly improved transportation systems within the last 60 years, the role of the warehouse has broadened. While at one time customers would accept delivery of an order two weeks after placing it, delivery now is often demanded within hours.

The modern warehouse has been forced to accept these rising expectations and changes have been necessary in order to meet them. The initial concern of someone seeking either a building site or an existing structure for establishing a warehouse facility is to determine the best market to be served and the optimum location whereby this market can be served.

In selecting a general warehouse location, the factors to be considered include:

- Quality and versatility of transportation
- Quantity and quality of labor
- Cost and quality of industrial land
- Taxes
- Utilities

Because of the close interrelationship between warehousing and transportation, the warehouse manager should consider the availability and quality of various transportation modes first and foremost in the decision making process.

Once the general location has been determined, the further task of deciding upon a particular building site must be confronted. As in the case of selecting a general location, again transportation is the single most important factor to be considered. Other important items to be taken into account are inherent location risks, services and taxes, carrier attitudes, facility design, and financing of the facility.

Since one of the major functions of the warehouse is to serve as a storage facility, the layout of the warehouse is a matter of great concern. The three major types of warehouse layout are cross-dock, L-shaped dock, and the single dock.

The cross-dock is generally considered to be the most efficient of the three. In this case, the receiving dock and the shipping dock are on opposite sides of the building allowing a traffic flow through the storage area from one dock to another. Merchandise arrives on an inbound truck; it is broken down into case or pallet unit loads, quickly sorted and then reshipped to its ultimate destination. Companies use cross-docking to minimize handling, storage costs, shrinkage, damage and product obsolescence. A visual representation of a cross-dock layout follows in figure 35. This great illustration comes from a November 1994 issue of Traffic Management magazine.

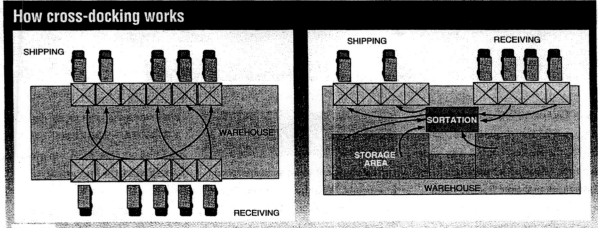

How cross-docking works

Figure 35 *Under a cross-docking system, palletloads can be moved directly across the warehouse floor from receiving to shipping (left). Boxes, however, first must pass through a sortation system (right).*

The L-shaped dock places the shipping doors at a ninety-degree angle to the receiving dock. The value of this set-up is that it minimizes travel time between docks. This is especially important in operations where pool distribution or freight consolidation is performed.

The single dock, as the name implies, combines both the receiving and shipping docks on the same wall of the facility. This is the simplest layout, but in many cases can result in excessive congestion.

Once the general layout has been decided upon, there are further, more detailed, layout considerations to be taken into account. Factors for concern include bulk storage provisions, order selection, high security, odor isolation, and temperature control.

One item of prime concern for the warehouse planner is the location, number and width of aisles. Aisle width is contingent upon the type of material handling system in use. A width of 12 feet is typically used for two-way traffic of forklifts. Narrow aisle equipment or angle stacking may allow this width to be reduced to about eight feet, and side-loading equipment will enable a further reduction to six feet.

The proper material handling equipment plays an important role in the efficient operation of any warehouse. There are many different systems you can choose from. In making a choice, the following criteria should be considered:

- Degree of flexibility required
- Type of job to be performed
- Amount of volume which will be handled
- Reliability of the proposed equipment
- Total cost involved

The simplest of handling systems are comprised of manually operated equipment. Larger operations generally require power equipment, the most common of which being the forklift truck. The modern forklift is a very versatile piece of equipment with a number of fork replacement attachments enabling it to perform a wide variety of functions. The attachments include the carton clamp, appliance handling devices, push-pull attachments, rotating clamps or forks, and crane booms.

The best of equipment will be of little value though, without proper maintenance and the training of personnel in correct usage of the equipment. You also must always keep in mind the future needs of the operation and any changes that might be required by expansion or diversification.

The warehouse manager, while in possession of the goods he is storing, is responsible for the security and condition of them. Because of the combustible nature of most inventories, the high risk of a fire is a major concern. This is made even worse by the difficulty of fighting one in highly stacked storage areas.

The most common fire fighting system in use is the automatic sprinkler system. There are two primary types of sprinkler systems - a wet pipe and a dry pipe. The dry pipe system uses air pressure in the sprinkler lines and a dry pipe valve where the water is held back by air. This use of air is a necessity for unheated buildings where pipes could freeze. When the sprinkler system is activated, the air pressure is released from the line to allow water to flow. In a wet pipe sprinkler system, water is under pressure in all sprinkler lines and is released immediately when the sprinklers are set-off. Therefore, the wet pipe system has a faster response time. Sprinkler systems vary in volume of water delivery and in the temperature setting at which sprinkler heads will open.

Other methods of fire fighting which some day may replace the sprinkler system include high-expansion foam that mixes detergent and water, creating an enormous amount of suds, filling the entire building, and thereby cutting off the oxygen supply to the fire and smothering it.

The other main concern of the warehouse manager is the possibility of theft and pilferage. The most common methods employed in stealing merchandise are:

- Breaking and entering the warehouse
- Theft by the warehouse employees
- Deliberate overloading of freight vehicles in collusion with outsiders
- Fraudulent preparation of warehouse releases

To minimize the possibility of breaking and entering, the grounds surrounding and the exterior of the building must be given great consideration. There should be sufficient lighting of the grounds and all possible entrances to the building. Appropriate fencing in, along with the cooperation of the local police or private security guards, will help control unauthorized admittance to the property.

Also, a proper alarm system will aid in reducing the incidents of breaking and entering. There are several types of electronic protection systems. The more popular ones include sound detectors, microwave sensors, and closed circuit television. Windows and doors should be equipped with electronic alarms. Two alternative means of protection are security guards or guard dogs inside of the building.

Probably the best way to counter theft and pilferage is by careful hiring and management of personnel. As warehouse manager, you should conduct a thorough background check of all prospective employees.

One way to guard against collusion theft is by careful supervision of truckers and other visitors to the warehouse. Another way is by the occasional ordering back of completed outbound loads for rechecking. If employees are aware that random checks and recalls are a possibility, they may be less likely to try and work some scam with outsiders.

In order to prevent theft through the use of fraudulent warehouse releases, tight clerical supervision is in order. Items to be considered include limiting access to blank forms used as warehouse releases, use of sequentially numbered forms, and limiting the number of people with authority to release goods.

There is no more serious waste in physical distribution than when finished goods are damaged prior to sale. Damage contributes unrecoverable cost resulting from wasted production, transportation, and warehousing, as well as repair and claim processing costs.

Damage can result from many conditions such as: inadequate packaging, mishandling in transit, or general carelessness while in storage. In many cases, due to human error, some of this damage must be considered inevitable.

Transportation damage occurs outside of the warehouse, but becomes the warehouse manager's problem if the damaged goods are accepted upon delivery. The most common causes of transportation related damage are abrasion from shifting within the vehicle, shock damage from bouncing or sudden starts and stops, leaks in the cargo body or in product containers, transfer handling damage, insufficient blocking and bracing, and bad loading practices.

However, not all damage occurs outside of the warehouse. Any warehousing operation will have its share of damages resulting from handling and storage operations. Forklifts cause damage when a load is dropped by a sudden stop, fast turn, or overloading. Forklift drivers, on occasion, will collide with stored material causing impact damage. Other common areas where damage occurs are at the corners of stacks, in narrow aisles, or at the face of a load if one load is pushed against another in the stacking process.

Stacking damage generally occurs when stack heights are greater than the packages are capable of holding. If package corners are not carefully aligned on pallets, or if entire stacks are not vertically aligned, stack strength is reduced and they may fall. Stacks may also fall from high humidity due to moisture's weakening effect upon corrugated packaging materials. Moisture damage may also occur as a result of roof or sprinkler leakage. Freezing is also a potential source of damage to merchandise. Goods in storage may also be damaged by odor transfer or chemical reaction.

All warehouse damage is a result of human error. It is inevitable that some damage will occur in all warehouses. This damage can come from inadequate training, poorly maintained handling equipment, improper communication of correct storage and handling practices, or ignorance of potential causes of contamination.

Controlling warehouse damage requires a proper attitude by all people involved, from the warehouse manager down through each picker and packer. Greater concern for damage can be developed through good record keeping and good communications.

Warehouse damage statistics should be developed which relate the pieces of merchandise damaged to the total pieces handled, to express a damage ratio. By making the warehouse personnel aware of the ratios at employee meetings and offering incentives to reduce them, interest in this subject will be intensified and hopefully the damage ratios will drop correspondingly.

One cause of damage is a result of management's decision to deliberately fill the warehouse in excess of its normal capacity. When overcrowding takes place, the monetary advantages gained from increased storage capacity must be weighed against the resultant damage or handling efficiency loss.

There are three major cost areas affecting the operation of a warehouse: storage costs, handling costs, and clerical costs. Several factors can affect these costs, and each of these factors is a variable, which will have a significant effect on the operation.

In calculating storage cost, the warehouse manager must consider three primary factors: space utilization, claim value, and specialized storage equipment. The first consideration in defining storage cost must be the realization that each square foot of warehouse space must yield a return. Therefore, the potential stacking height and stacking efficiency of the goods to be stored must be determined.

In many cases, specialized storage equipment must be used to obtain desired efficiency of cube utilization. Pallet racks, tier racks, bins, and shelving are examples of equipment designed to increase stacking height and storage.

The prime elements affecting handling costs are:

- Hourly labor costs
- Material handling equipment
- Their combined productivity

Productivity is ordinarily defined in terms of the number of pieces, pallet loads or pounds, which under normal circumstances can be handled per man-hour. This is obviously the primary calculation in determining handling costs and it is also the element that is subject to the widest variations. Therefore, it must be constantly rechecked as the warehouse operation progresses.

When developing handling costs you must consider the elements of warehouse handling in sequence, and then develop associated times for each element. The elements to be measured are receiving, in-storage operations, and shipping.

In considering receiving, you must determine whether the goods arrive in palletized or unitized form or if they arrive loose. Will the truck drivers assist in unloading and palletizing? How many line items are in the load, and are they segregated or mixed? All of these questions must be answered to determine the cost of receiving.

In-storage costs include inspection and repacking of damage, consolidation of stock to reduce wasted space, establishment of order selection lines and restocking of these lines, rotation of stocks, or repackaging. These are costs incurred while the goods are in the warehouse.

In considering shipping, again it must be determined if unitization is employed. Goods that are received unitized are generally shipped in smaller quantities. You must also consider the average order size, both in number of pieces and number of line items. If order picking, broken case shipping, or repackaging will be required, you must also determine the cost of each of these elements of the shipping operation. To determine the cost of shipping, you must then total the costs of each of these separate elements.

Then the elements of receiving, in-storage operations and shipping are added together to develop a total handling cost.

Two factors govern clerical cost:

- Number of documents processed
- Degree of complexity of the documents

The degree of automation is also an important factor in clerical costs. If you operation is largely manual, your clerical costs will be significantly higher than if you fully embrace computer technology.

In the clerical function, the elements to be considered in determining the total cost include cost of preparing receiving documents, inventory reports, and shipping documents. Cost of communications and computer equipment must be calculated. The sum of these elements is the total clerical cost.

The net result of all these calculations is the determination of a storage cost per unit per month, a per unit handling cost, and a cost for clerical services. Such costs should be determined whether the operation is public, contract, or private. It is the only way in which the general efficiency of the warehouse operation can be measured and checked.

Considering what we just discussed, I think it is quite apparent that there is more to running a warehouse efficiently than just having storage space. To operate a warehouse you must be familiar with all aspects of business, or depending upon the size of the operation, have a very competent staff of subordinates. The service performed by the warehouse is a vital and rewarding one and should be entered into only with the best of preparation.

Shipping/Receiving

Shipping and receiving are two of the most common warehouse activities. The functions are closely interrelated and in most companies they are part of the same department. Some of the most typical receiving functions provided by warehouse personnel are:

- Schedule delivery appointments.
- Control the movement and activity of delivering drivers.
- Properly secure the delivery trailer to the loading dock.
- Check trailer seal on full loads for signs of tampering.
- Unload freight and maintain accurate count.
- Reconcile delivery documents against actual counts.
- Record any exceptions on the carrier delivery receipt.
- Photograph any damages to freight as a method of documentation to substantiate any freight claims.
- Perform quality checks on incoming goods.
- Assign incoming goods to a warehouse location.
- Put-away incoming goods into their designated warehouse location.

Shipping is largely the opposite of receiving. Shipping personnel may have the responsibility pulling the correct merchandise from their respective inventory location, preparing shipping documents, contacting the carrier for pick-up of the outgoing goods, loading the freight on the truck, verifying the shipping count, etc.

Auto Identification

Introduction

Automatic Identification (Auto ID) is a collection of interrelated technologies that allow for automated collection of data. The most common types of Auto ID that are currently in use are bar coding, radio frequency ID, radio frequency data communication and voice data collection. For the purpose of this chapter, we are mainly concerned with bar coding and radio frequency technologies.

I will spare you the gory technological details and try to concentrate on how this technology is a benefit to a typical warehouse operation.

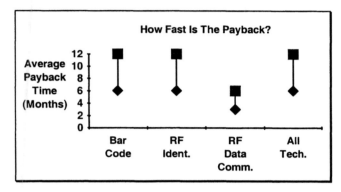

A common management concern is what the payback will be on technology such as this because it certainly will involve a sizable capital outlay. So I don't lose your interest right away, let me assure you that payback comes within a very reasonable period of time.

Source: Automatic Identification Manufacturers Inc.

As you can see from the chart, regardless of the technology, the average system pays for itself within six to 12 months.

The benefits of Auto ID

Auto ID, for the purpose of this chapter, will be for the most part confined to a discussion of bar coding. Radio frequency identification, one popular method of providing real-time data collection of bar coded data will be touched on as well. Other methods of data collection such as batch data terminals will be discussed too.

Reduced to their minimum, the advantages of bar codes are that they are quick and accurate. This may sound very simplistic but the impact of these two factors is dramatic.

When implemented to their fullest, bar codes can replace manual data entry, provide for transportable data and increase data accuracy and reliability over manual methods by phenomenal amounts.

As an example, key-entry results in an error rate of one in every 300 characters entered. Bar codes have an error rate of one in every 1,000,000 characters entered. The American Management Association, way back in 1980, estimated that the cost of an error was $27.00. For example, if a company enters 1,000,000 characters of data per year, which is probably very conservative, and you accept the manual error rate of one in every 300 characters, then this sample company makes 3,333 errors per year. At the rate of $27.00 per error, this is a cost of $90,000.00. Bar coding could eliminate this cost in one year's time!

In addition to the monetary savings there is the accuracy improvement. When implemented properly, bar coding could virtually eliminate order picking errors, inventory put-away errors and receiving errors. Due to the reduction of these types of errors, inventory integrity and accuracy would be greatly enhanced.

The use of bar codes and laser scanners can significantly improve the taking of physical inventory. By using this technology the amount of time required for a full physical inventory can be greatly reduced and can also make viable the option of regular cycle counts as a replacement for an annual full count.

By improving accuracy and increasing speed a company can achieve not only the internal benefits described above, but additionally can move closer to achieving total customer satisfaction.

Here is a list of the potential gains derived from implementing an Auto ID system.

Inventory
- Reduce levels of raw materials, work-in-process & finished goods
- Trim inventory shrinkage
- Improve inventory availability when needed
- Cut time required to find inventory
- Reduce obsolete inventory

Labor
- Improve worker & supervisor productivity levels
- Reduce paper handling
- Cut data entry time
- Trim time required to take physical inventory
- Reduce data reentry in other departments
- Reduce expediting efforts

Production
- Reduce lead times
- Trim scrap levels
- Cut rework
- Standardize operations
- Boost machine utilization through improved scheduling
- Reduce time to fill orders

Customer Service
- Improve on-time deliveries
- Higher quality levels
- Reduce customer complaints
- Trim shipping errors
- Better product tracking after shipment

- Able to pinpoint order status for customers at any time
- Greater flexibility and responsiveness to customer requests

Management Decision Making
- Better-organized database
- Elimination of uncertainty in knowing inventory status and location
- Access to more timely information
- Better real-time decision-making

Financial
- Reduce dollar days for inventory
- Outstanding bills reduced due to higher customer satisfaction
- Better cash flow position

What should be bar coded

Ultimately, a company should strive to bar code the entire distribution process. Using technology such as electronic data interchange (EDI), bar coding becomes part of the cycle from the time the purchase order is placed with the vendor, continuing until the product is shipped to the customer. Each step along the way involves coding product and scanning to provide accurate, real-time traceability.

To effect a system such as this requires a major overhaul of the way a company does business and should not be implemented in one fell swoop. The most efficient method is to set-up an implementation schedule that involves bar coding different aspects of the process in stages.

A feasible implementation schedule follows:

1. Bar code inventory

2. Customer Order Fulfillment

3. Shipping
- Shipment Labels
- Shipment Tracking

4. Receiving
- Bar Code Incoming Product at Dock
- Scan for Receipt to Dock

5. Production
- Manufacturing Order (M.O.) Issuance
- Product Tracking

6. Purchasing

- ♦ Purchase Order Placement
- ♦ Vendor Labeling of Product

A hypothetical scenario

Here is an example of a fully functioning Auto ID system in action.

1. Incoming goods

A purchase order is issued to a vendor accompanied by bar code labels for the product and the shipping container. The goods arrive at the loading dock and the bar coded label on the shipping container is scanned via a hand held RF or batch scanner for the purchase order number. In so doing, the purchase order details, which can be down-loaded to a batch scanner or can be accessed through radio frequency directly, are now available to the operator on the dock. The shipping container is opened and each bar coded item in the container is scanned. If RF technology is used then the order is immediately received to dock. If batch scanners are used then, whenever the data in the scanner is uploaded to the main computer system, the goods are received. The goods can then pass to quality control (QC) where the same process is repeated. Finally they are scanned one more time for receipt to stock.

2. Customer Order Fulfillment/Production Parts Issuance

A bar coded customer order pick list or manufacturing order is issued and given to an order picker. The order picker scans the sales order or manufacturing order number via a hand held RF or batch scanner. The order details, through the same means as described above, are then available to the picker. The picker is then guided by the program in the scanner to the appropriate locations and prompted for the part numbers and quantities to pick. Along the way locations and part numbers are scanned. Any incorrect picks will be rejected by the scanner, preventing picking errors. As well, through this process, inventory is adjusted on a real-time basis.

3. Physical Inventory

Through the use of hand-held scanners, inventory counters scan locations and input quantities. The software in the scanner then compares counts and determines whether re-counts are required. Once counts are determined as correct, inventory is adjusted accordingly. All this is accomplished without manually comparing physical counts to computer counts.

4. Miscellaneous

- Shipping containers are bar coded with customer P.O. # and assorted other information to allow customer to take advantage of bar code technology or to meet customer requirements.

- All scanned bar code transactions are date- and time-stamped. Scanning stages of production aid in the implementation of a cost accounting system.

- Scanning serial numbered items providing traceability for item location, warranty purposes, etc.

- With bar coding in place, adding electronic data interchange (EDI) capabilities are facilitated.

- Bar coded employee ID tags provide better time management and eliminates the need for time cards/sheets.

- Bar codes are used for asset management providing better control of expensive equipment.

- Bar coding of engineering and other critical files provides better document control.

The cost of Auto ID

Well, now that you know what Auto ID can do and how it can help a company's operation, it is time to tell you what it is going to cost. There are two groups of costs involved: start-up costs and ongoing costs.

Start-up Costs

- System Design
- Orientation & Training of Personnel
- Label Redesign
- Packaging Changes
- Printer Hardware
- Bar Code Reading Hardware
- Terminal Hardware
- Verification Tool Hardware
- Applicator Hardware (if employed)
- Work Center Computer Hardware
- Work Center Computer Software
- Host Computer System Change Cost

Ongoing Costs

- Manual Application (if no applicator)
- Labels & Supplies

- Hardware Maintenance
- Software Maintenance

A recent survey conducted by the Automatic Identification Manufacturers Inc. (AIM) has

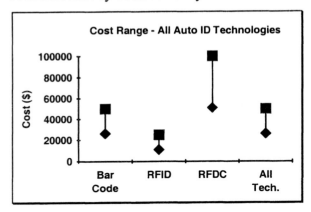

identified the average costs incurred in implementing various types of Auto ID systems. As you can see from the chart, the AIM survey has found that the average Auto ID system, including hardware and software, is valued at $26,000 to $50,000. As well, the average system pays for itself within six to 12 months.

This survey also asked its respondents to identify the costs of bar code technology by application. You can see from the chart

below how the cost of bar coding is broken down by application.

The average cost of all bar code applications is $26,000 to $50,000. The most expensive

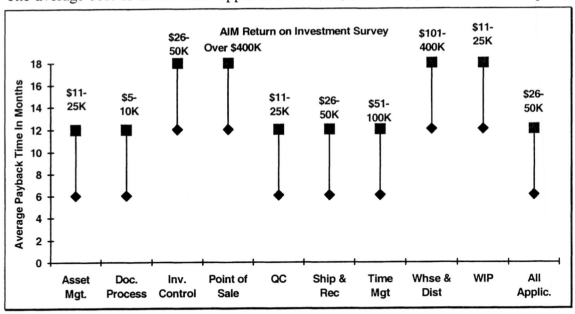

application is point-of-sale systems with an average cost of $400,000. However, even with such a high set-up cost, POS systems have a payback period of only 12 to 18 months. The least expensive application is document tracking with an average cost of $5,000 to $10,000.

Conclusion

Well, that pretty much covers the basics of Auto ID. The technology is mature and some clear-cut standards have emerged so there is very little risk in adopting it. In fact, in a few years Auto ID will no longer be considered state-of-the-art but merely the way business is done. Ultimately, the technology will have to be adopted.

Inventory Management

In order to manage a warehouse properly, it is essential that you have a reasonable understanding of inventory management principles. What will follow is the fifty-cent tour of the essentials of inventory management.

There are three primary inventory control approaches. These are:

- Cyclical Ordering System
- Order Point or Fixed-Order Quantity System
- Material Requirements Planning (MRP)

A cyclical ordering system is time-based. Items are ordered to accommodate anticipated usage for a given period of time. Orders can be placed with a supplier so you receive a predetermined amount at a fixed interval, such as every two weeks, every month, etc. With this system, actual on-hand stocks must be periodically monitored to ensure that the timing and quantities established are accurate. If not, adjustments need to be made.

The order point system is based on order points and order quantities, instead of time. Typically, minimum and maximum levels for a given item are determined, as well as a minimal safety stock, just in case. Ordering is planned so the inventory will not exceed the maximum nor fall below the minimum levels established. Hopefully, the following illustration will make the concept clear.

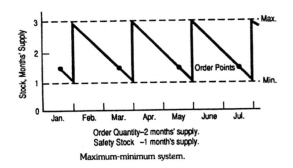

Order Quantity–2 months' supply.
Safety Stock –1 month's supply.

Maximum-minimum system.

Material Requirements Planning (MRP) is a computerized method of managing production inventories. The basic premise is that, once a company's master production schedule is developed and all product bills of material are finalized, it is possible to precisely calculate material requirements for a particular period of operation. Production material requirements are typically analyzed weekly, but in advance of the actual need. The MRP system then generates requisitions for required materials with an expected arrival several days prior to the actual manufacturing need date.

MRP is a complex process requiring significant computer resources. A one paragraph thumbnail sketch does not do the topic justice, but I thought it at least needed to be mentioned.

ABC Analysis

Remember way back to the beginning of this book? We talked about something called Pareto's Law or the 80-20 Rule. Don't believe me? Go ahead, turn back to page three. It's there. Anyway, Pareto reappears in analyzing your inventory. What you will typically find is that 20% of your inventory items account for 80% of your total inventory investment. By investigating further, you will probably find that 10% of your inventory's items account for 75% of the investment and 25% of the items make-up 90% of the total investment. The remaining 75% of the items account for only 10% of the inventory investment. Performing this exercise on your inventory is called an ABC analysis. It identifies areas of focus for different classes of inventory.

EOQ

EOQ is a mathematical formula for calculating the most cost effective order size for a purchase. It is based on the premise *that the lowest annual total cost occurs at the order quantity where inventory carrying costs equal acquisition costs*. To explain some terms, **carrying costs** include:

- Opportunity costs of investment funds
- Insurance costs
- Property taxes
- Storage costs
- Obsolescence and deterioration

Acquisition costs include:

- Percentage of wages and operating expenses associated with the purchase.
- Costs of supplies such as forms for purchasing, production control, receiving, etc.
- Costs of services such as telephone, fax, postage, etc.

Incremental costs are those costs that actually change as a result of making a particular operating decision.

The calculation has the following variables:

Q = Order quantity
A = Incremental acquisition cost per order
I = Annual incremental inventory carrying costs
U= Expected annual usage
C = Delivered unit cost of the material

The formula is listed below:

$$Q = \sqrt{\frac{2UA}{IC}}$$

Visually, EOQ can be illustrated as in the following graph:

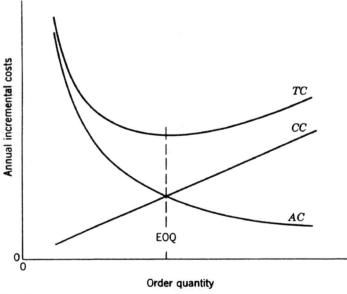

FIGURE 36
Relationship of indirect material costs to order quantity. (*AC* = incremental acquisition costs; *CC* = incremental carrying costs; *TC* = total incremental costs.)

Let's do a quick example. A manufacturer wants to know the EOQ for widgets. We can plug the following numbers into the formula and see what we come up with.

A = $50 acquisition cost per order
I = 25% inventory carrying costs
U = 100,000 piece annual usage
C = $20 delivered cost per unit

EOQ = sqrt((2 x 100,000 x 50)/(.25x20))
EOQ = sqrt(10,000,000/5)
EOQ = sqrt(2,000,000)
EOQ = 1,414

All right, this may be more math than some of you really want to contend with. I know it requires some mental gymnastics but the concept is important and useful.

Using EOQ in managing inventories can:

- Minimize indirect material costs
- Yield frequent small-quantity, high-value orders
- Yield infrequent large-quantity, lower-cost orders

One warning though, EOQ is of little use when dealing with materials whose prices or usage fluctuate radically or with materials whose usage cannot be predicted with a reasonable degree of accuracy.

JIT

Just-In-Time is one of the most overly used business buzz-words of the last 15 years or so. Consequently, there are many different opinions about what this concept really means. One of the more succinct definitions I have found is as follows:

Just-In-Time is the practice that requires the consumption of resources at the last possible moment relative to production for customer demand. This requires the elimination of all waste. Waste is defined as all the non-value added activities that take place in the total manufacturing, distribution and purchasing processes.

The implementation of a JIT system requires, in many cases, an alteration of the conventional corporate mind set. For example, contrast the difference in philosophy between the traditional approach and the JIT mentality on a number of key issues:

Issue	Conventional Wisdom	Just-In-Time
Bottom Line	Cost Reduction.	Margin maximization.
Quality vs. Cost	Least cost with "acceptable quality."	Top, consistent quality; zero defects.
Inventories	Large inventories (quantity purchase discounts, manufacturing economies of scale, safety stock).	Low inventories with reliable, continuous-flow delivery.
Flexibility	Long "minimum" lead times; minimal flexibility.	Short lead times; customer-service driven; great flexibility.
Transportation	Least cost within "acceptable service levels."	Totally reliable service levels.
Vendor negotiations	Tough, adversarial negotiations.	Joint-venture "partnerships."
Number of vendors	Many; avoid single source.	Few; long-term, open relationship.
Vendor communications	Minimal; many secrets; tightly controlled.	Open; sharing of information; joint problem solving.
General	Cost driven.	Customer-Service driven.

The emphasis of a JIT program is on reduced inventories, frequent shipments and short delivery lead times. Consequently, management must adopt a "pull" method of inventory control that features high inventory turns and low safety stocks. This is just the opposite of the conventional "push" system where inventory is stockpiled.

Just-In-Time methods should not be applied in all circumstances and with all vendors. It is important to fully research the ramifications of implementation and proceed only in areas where it makes economic sense.

Just-In-Time also does not work well within the rigid hierarchical boundaries of the traditional corporate structure. For a JIT system to work you need close cooperation among Engineering, Manufacturing, Purchasing, Inventory, Transportation and Warehousing. A cross-functional team approach works best.

Implementation of a JIT system is a painstaking process that cannot happen overnight. The necessary alliances must be built with key vendors and carriers participating in the program. As well, the information technology required to provide real-time data on manufacturing needs must be in place.

According to the JIT experts, there is a five-phase guideline to follow for implementation of such a system. The phases include:

- *Phase I:* "Cleaning up" the operations.
- *Phase II:* Effecting a company-wide culture change.
- *Phase III:* Preparing logistics for JIT.
- *Phase IV:* Implementing the program.

- *Phase V:*   Reviewing and monitoring after implementation.

It is evident that there are no short-cuts to a successful Just-In-Time program. Each step must be properly executed for the program to run smoothly. In order to consider such a program there must be commitment from the highest levels of management to follow through on the necessary steps to make it work. Without that support it cannot happen.

Chapter 4

Computers and Logistics

Introduction

It is truly amazing how, since the release of the first mass-market microcomputers in 1977, these machines have progressed from essentially high-priced toys for the hobbyist to such a dominant force in the business world. In many companies, it is not unusual to find a PC on every desk.

The logistics department was among the last to join the personal computer bandwagon. The main reason for this is that, in general, we had the tendency to be relegated to the corporate back seat and as such, it was thought that we had no need for such high priced perks. However, times have changed and the corporate powers that be have realized that the distribution department can save a sizable sum of money and that by utilizing the power of the computer this task can be significantly facilitated.

In the pages that follow, I would like to clear up some of the confusion surrounding personal computers and perhaps make them seem a little less formidable to the non-initiated.

I'll start out by explaining, in non-technical terms, how computers work. From there, some history on the origins and the progression of microcomputers will be presented. We shall offer a detailed discussion of computer languages; the instructions that enable these machines to perform the tasks that they do. After that, the discussion will turn to general application programs, such as spreadsheets, data base managers, word processing programs and so on. We will then move on to a discussion of some of the more technical aspects of personal computing, that being local area networks and electronic data interchange.

Finally, we will take a brief look at transportation and distribution specific applications for the personal computer. We shall cover many different aspects of how the computer can be applied to solving our specific problems.

We will initially take a look at the how the microcomputer can be applied within the overall scheme of things in the logistics department. Then we will take a look at some of the specific types of software packages that are available to solve the problems encountered by the logistics professional. The categories that will be covered include motor carrier rating, warehousing, and import/export documentation management.

I hope that by the time one manages to work his way through these pages, those who were unfamiliar with the ins and outs of microcomputing will be somewhat better off than when they began.

How PCs Operate

The typical PC consists of four basic functional units -- the central processing unit, secondary storage, input devices and output devices.

The central processing unit (CPU), also frequently termed the system unit, is where the actual computing takes place. This is where you will find the microprocessor, the tiny silicon chip within which the instructions that orchestrate all of the functions of the machine are received, processed and dispatched.

Microprocessors have advanced markedly since the debut of the Intel 8080 and Motorola 6800 way back in 1974. These chips enabled the microcomputer revolution to get its start. They are both termed 8-bit chips.

A bit is the smallest single unit of data that can be represented within the computer. A bit represents a particular binary state within the computer -- electrical current is either present or absent; gates are either open or closed; magnetic materials in the magnetic cores of some secondary storage devices are magnetized either in one direction or the opposite. This is why binary numbers (base two) are the basis of all computer programming. Continuous streams of zeros and ones are the means by which computers do their thing, so to speak.

The alphabetical and numerical characters appearing on a typical computer keyboard are represented by eight bit groups called bytes. The coding system utilized by microcomputers to represent these characters is known as ASCII (American Standard Code for Information Interchange). For example, the capital letter 'A' is represented by the binary number 01000001; the dollar sign '$' is represented by the binary number 00100100; and the symbol for the number '5' is represented by 00110101.

Anyway, an 8-bit microprocessor processes data eight bits at a time. What this means is that data is passed into, through and out of the microprocessor in eight bit chunks. The microprocessor contains a number of registers, units of high speed memory. In an 8-bit microprocessor the registers are eight bits wide. As well, the data path, the number of bits that a microprocessor can fetch from or store to memory at one time, is also eight bits. A few examples of popular 8-bit microprocessors are the Intel 8080, Zilog Z80 and MOS Technology 6502.

The next generation of microprocessors was 16-bit processors. These have 16-bit registers and data paths. Representative of this class of microprocessor is the Intel 8086, 80186 and 80286. The Intel 8088, used in the original IBM PC, is a hybrid chip. It contains 16-bit registers but an 8-bit data path. The reason for this design was to preserve compatibility with peripherals originally manufactured for older 8-bit computers.

The current state of the art in microprocessors is the 32-bit processor. The first examples of 32-bit chips in mass-market PCs were the Intel 80386 and the Motorola 68020 and 68030 microprocessors. As there was in the case of the 16-bit chips, there were hybrids in the 32-bit world as well. The Motorola 68000, the brains behind the original Apple Macintosh, had 32-bit registers but a 16-bit data path. The Intel 80386SX, once used in IBM PC compatible machines was a hybrid also with the same set up as the 68000. 32-bit microprocessors have evolved over the past eight or so years into some formidable powerhouses. The current state-of-the-art in 32-bit processors is the Intel Pentium 4, the AMD Athlon and the Motorola PowerPC.

The performance of a microprocessor is usually measured in terms of clock speed and word width. Clock speed is the speed at which the microprocessor operates. This is measured in megahertz (MHz) or gigahertz (GHz), which represents millions or billions of operations per second. So, a computer operating at a clock speed of 1 GHz is capable of executing 1 billion operations a second. The second criterion of performance measurement, word width, relates back to what we previously discussed regarding register size and data path width. For example, in the Intel family of microprocessors the 8080 had a word width of 8-bits, the 80286 had a word width of 16-bits and the 80386, 80486 and Pentium line has a word width of 32-bits.

Also within the CPU, you would find the computer's memory. This is where programs and data can be stored and acted upon by the microprocessor. Memory is divided into two different types -- read-only memory (ROM) and random access memory (RAM).

Read-only memory is that which contains instructions to the computer that, under normal circumstances, cannot be altered. It is static and remains after the power to the computer has been turned off. ROM typically contains such items as built-in programming languages and operating systems -- both of which shall be discussed subsequently.

Random access memory is the memory in which people run their computer programs. It can be read from and written to by the user. RAM however is volatile, once the power is turned off, what was once in memory is transformed into cosmic dust.

Memory is divided into addresses. Each address has the potential to contain one instruction or one piece of data. The typical business PC's memory contains in the neighborhood of 64,000,000 of these addresses. However, they can contain anywhere between 16,000,000 and 128,000,000 addresses, or sometimes even greater.

In the early days, memory was measured in kilobytes or thousands of bytes. The letter 'K' for kilo represented this. So, when some of the early machines were termed as having 64K of memory, that meant that they had 64,000 memory addresses. Today, memory is customarily measured in terms of millions of bytes, with each byte representing an address. The letters 'Mb' for megabyte symbolizes this. The computer in-crowd refers to these as "megs". Therefore, your typical business PC with 64,000,000 memory addresses, is said to have 64Mb of memory. This is how memory is measured in common parlance.

Secondary storage is utilized for several purposes. It can be used to augment the main memory within the CPU. It can also be employed to store programs and data not currently being utilized by the CPU. Lastly, it can be used as an input and/or output device.

Secondary storage on a business PC generally takes the form of disk or tape drives, or compact disks (CD) like those used for audio purposes. Disk drives are either floppy disk drives or hard disk drives. The magnetic disk medium used closely resembles that of a phonograph record. Each disk is covered by hundreds of concentric tracks, all of which can contain data. The data is represented on the disk, as alluded to earlier, in the form of spots that are magnetized in either one direction or another, and symbolized by a binary zero or one. When the disk is accessed it rotates and the data is either written to or read from the disk surface by a read/write drive head.

Floppy disks are typically 3 ½ inches in diameter. The storage capacity of these disks is generally 1.44Mb in IBM PC format.

Hard disks, once called Winchester disks, offer much greater convenience, speed and storage capacity to the user than do floppy disks. Large application programs like word processors, spreadsheets or data bases are impossible to run without one. Hard disks usually start at about 3Gb (gigabytes, gigs, or billions of bytes) in capacity and currently can offer up to in excess of 50Gb. The performance of a hard disk is generally judged in terms of average access time. Access time is measured in milliseconds. The hard disk on the original IBM PCXT had an average access time of about 90 milliseconds (ms). Now it is typical to have hard disks that will run below 8 ms.

Input devices are those that transmit data to the CPU for processing. They generally take instructions in a humanly intelligible form and translate them into machine intelligible form. However, they can merely transfer instructions from one machine intelligible form to another. The most commonly thought of input device would be the computer keyboard. Other types of input devices are disk or tape drives, CD drives, optical scanners, DVD drives and bar code readers.

Output devices perform the reverse operation of input devices. Types of output devices include the cathode-ray tube (CRT) - the screen one views while operating the computer, printers, CDs, and disk or tape drives.

There are four major types of printers currently in use for business applications: dot-matrix, daisy wheel, ink-jet and laser printers.

Dot-matrix printers utilize an impact technology. A group of wires in a print head, usually 18 or 24, are fired, thereby striking a ribbon and releasing ink on the paper as the print head moves the length of the line. The density of the dots affects the quality of the output. These are usually used for printing multi-part forms.

Daisy wheel printers are also impact printers. They utilize a flat disk with petal-like projections. On the end of each projection a character is embossed. The daisy wheel rotates to select the appropriate character that then strikes a ribbon to print the character on the paper. Daisy wheel printers produce fully formed characters that are equal in quality to that of any office typewriter. These printers however, are generally much slower and noisier than their dot-matrix counterparts. While once quite common, these are not seen too often anymore.

Ink-jet printers employ a non-contact technology. The print head contains a number of nozzles that are connected to a reservoir of ink. From these nozzles the ink is propelled to the paper, creating characters and patterns. Ink-jet printers have become immensely popular over the past several years. They are an excellent choice for providing high-quality color and black-and-white output at a reasonable cost.

The last major category of business printers is laser printers. The center of a laser printer is a drum coated with a photoelectric substance that develops a positive or negative charge in response to light. A laser beam is aimed at a rotating mirror that scans the beam across the face of the drum, turning on and off according to the digital information coming from the image. The result is an electrostatic image of the page on the drum. As the drum rotates it passes over a reservoir of toner. The charged sections of the drum attract and retain the toner. This toner-laden image on the drum is then brought in contact with a piece of paper. The toner, through electrical attraction, attaches itself to the paper. Heated rollers then bond the toner to the paper to create the final image on the page. This completed page is then ejected into an output tray.

The History of Computers (primarily personal computers)

If one thinks about it, it is truly remarkable how far technology has advanced since the first digital computer was introduced in 1946. The ENIAC (Electronic Numerical Integrator And Calculator) was designed and built at the University of Pennsylvania. It weighed 30-tons and took up 1500 square feet of floor space. The first computer developed in Europe was the EDSAC (Electronic Delay-Storage Automatic Computer). This machine was built at Cambridge University in 1949.

What characterized these earliest machines is that the switching and control functions were handled by vacuum tubes. This feature typifies what is termed the first-generation of computers. EDSAC had one feature that ENIAC lacked. Within the computer was stored the instructions to control the machine and the data to be operated upon. This was the first of the stored program computers. The first commercially available digital computer was the Sperry Rand UNIVAC I. This was sold to the Bureau of the Census and put in place in 1951.

In the late 1950s, the bulky and hot vacuum tubes were replaced in computer designs by smaller, more reliable solid-state transistors. The use of transistors as the basic component of computer design characterizes what is known as the second generation of computers.

1963 brought about the start of third-generation computers. Solid-logic technology (SLT) enabled the development of the integrated circuit (IC). ICs allowed the placement of as many as 664 transistors, diodes and other associated components on a silicon chip less than one eighth of an inch square.

We are now in the midst of the fourth-generation of computers. Characterized by continued miniaturization of circuitry, such developments as large-scale integration (LSI) and very large-scale integration (VLSI) have enabled the current crop of machines to have a level of power and speed that was almost unimaginable 20 years ago.

Now on to the history of the microcomputer. The first commercially available personal computer was the Scelbi-8H that went on sale in March 1974. The machine was designed around the Intel 8008 microprocessor, a less powerful 8-bit design than the later 8080. A machine in kit form with 1K of memory sold for $440.00. About 200 of these machines were sold in kit form and assembled. Half were the Scelbi-8H hobby machines, the rest were Scelbi-8B business computers, which were released in April 1975, having as much as 16K of memory.

The first commercially successful microcomputer was the MITS Altair 8800 designed by Ed Roberts. It was introduced to the world as a cover story in the January 1975 issue of Popular Electronics. The Altair used the already mentioned Intel 8080 8-bit microprocessor. The most basic kit version was offered for sale at $397.00. A completely assembled and tested version sold for $498.00. However, what you got for your money was not a whole lot. What you did get was a blue and white box that housed a motherboard, a front panel with switches and lights indicating register contents, the power supply and 16 expansion slots. It came with no standard amount of memory or interfaces.

The minimum usable configuration was an 8K system that MITS sold for $995.00. In addition to this you also needed a cassette interface and recorder, and a terminal. Therefore, a truly complete 8K system actually cost you about $1900.00. MITS sold thousands of Altairs. One of the features that made it a success and characterized most other successful future designs was its open architecture.

Those 16 expansion slots made possible a wealth of alternatives that the designers of the machine could never have imagined. They allowed for growth and diversification of the machine, spawned another complete industry of add-on board developers and manufacturers, and in so doing essentially guaranteed the success of the product.

In addition to having the distinction of being the first commercially successful microcomputer, the Altair 8800 is also responsible for most of what we associate with microcomputers beyond the basic hardware itself. For example, the Altair User's Group was formed by MITS in 1975. That same year an Altair newsletter began publication. In March 1976, the MITS 1st World Altair Computer Convention (WACC) was held. The WACC holds the honor of being the first major microcomputer convention. The first retail computer outlets were set-up to sell Altairs. The open architecture enabled the rise of the add-on board industry. And finally, the high-level computer language chosen by Ed Roberts to be used with the machine was none other than the version of BASIC developed by Paul Allen and Bill Gates from a new company called Microsoft.

The next major development in the evolution of the microcomputer was the beginning of Apple Computer. In 1976, Steve Wozniak, a technician at Hewlett-Packard, attended Wescon (an electronics trade show) and purchased a few of the MOS Technology 6502 chips that were selling for $20.00 a piece. With this he wrote a BASIC language interpreter and then followed-up in the spring of 1976 at the Homebrew Computer Club with the Apple I.

The Apple I really wasn't a whole lot to write home about. It had no keyboard, no power supply and no case. It did however, impress Steve Jobs who was willing to form a company with Wozniak to sell the machines. It also impressed Paul Terrell who had in the previous year opened the first Byte Shop, a computer-related retail outlet, in Mountain

View, CA. Terrell placed an order for 50 of the machines. Within the first few months of the venture, Wozniak and Jobs had managed to sell about 200 machines to retailers in the Bay Area at a price of $666.00 a piece.

What really got the company off the ground was not the quality of the merchandise however, fine as it may have been, but the interest of A. C. 'Mike' Markkula. Markkula was an engineer who had also gotten a significant amount of business experience while working for Intel. Stock options with Intel had made him a millionaire and he retired at age 34. Markkula visited Wozniak and Jobs in their garage one day and was converted. After a few months, Markkula put up $91,000.00 of his own money and took an active role in the venture. He hired Mike Scott as president and within five years Apple was in the Fortune 500.

The next major event in this chronicle occurred in 1977. It was in that year that three new microcomputer systems were introduced which started the industry in the direction we are now taking. At the first West Coast Computer Faire on April 15, the Commodore PET and the Apple II were presented, and on August 3 in New York the Radio Shack TRS-80 Model I was announced. By the fall of 1977, all three machines were shipping.

Prior to the release of these machines, most people who purchased microcomputers bought them in kit form. Usually you could buy a kit for 25 to 30 percent less than the assembled version. With the arrival of these machines the emphasis went in the direction of the assembled systems.

The Apple II, packaged in a molded plastic case, with BASIC in ROM, color graphics, an 8-bit 6502 processor and 4K of RAM cost $1298.00. The machine was equipped with eight expansion slots and became one of the most successful of microcomputers. The PET was designed by Chuck Peddle, formerly of MOS Technology, and like the Apple used the MOS 6502 microprocessor. The TRS-80 Model I was offered with 4K of memory, an uppercase only display capability, a limited version of BASIC and a cassette interface. It originally listed as an assembled machine for $399.00.

1978 saw the next major advance in microcomputer technology. In that year both Apple and Radio Shack introduced 5 1/4 inch disk drives. Anyone who has ever used cassette input/output (I/O), and I have, will know well what an improvement disk drives offered. This development also brought about the arrival of a multitude of software. Floppy drives made possible software that never could have existed without them.

The next major development in the evolution of the microcomputer was the debut of the IBM PC in 1981. Big Blue did not break any new ground with its machine. In fact they followed very closely to the plan set by Apple. This included an open architecture. They provided five expansion slots to allow for extensive modification and customization of the basic machine. IBM also made available to developers a full set of electrical schematics for the computer and a printout and explanation of the ROM-based Basic Input/Output System (BIOS) which provides the hooks into the machine for hardware and software.

IBM approached Bill Gates of Microsoft for a package of languages for their new machine. Being unfamiliar with the microcomputer industry, they also approached Gates for the rights to CP/M, the current industry standard operating system for microcomputers. Gates informed them that CP/M (Control Program for Microcomputers) was not his product, but that they should talk to Gary Kildall of Digital Research Corporation. Digital Research (formerly Intergalactic Digital Research) refused to sign IBM's nondisclosure agreement and so they went back to Microsoft to see if they could develop an operating system for them. Well, they did and the result was the ubiquitous PC-DOS (MS-DOS in the generic form marketed by Microsoft).

When the original IBM PC was introduced in August 1981 it came equipped with a 8/16-bit Intel 8088 microprocessor operating at a clock speed of 4.77 MHz, 16K of RAM and a cassette interface and sold for $1265.00, $1565.00 with a Color/Graphics display adapter (CGA). A serious system configured to compete with an Apple II+ came with 48K RAM, one 160K floppy disk drive, PC-DOS and a CGA board. This would set you back $2630.00, slightly less than a 48K Apple II+.

The impact of the IBM PC on the microcomputer industry was unprecedented. This machine and its so-called clones, all utilizing the MS-DOS operating system and some variation on the Intel 8086/88 family of microprocessors, have thoroughly dominated the business market. IBM compatibility became almost essential for a machine to have any success as a business system. In addition, hundreds of manufacturers of add-on boards, IBM specific software and clones owe their very existence to the revolution that this essentially mediocre machine started.

On January 24, 1984, the next major element in the evolution of the microcomputer was introduced: the Apple Macintosh. This diminutive computer didn't resemble anything currently considered normal in the world of personal computers.

The Mac, as it soon became called, was certainly an innovation. Just about everything about it was different from the norm. The machine had a nine inch high-resolution, black and white monitor; 128K of RAM that was not expandable; a single 400K - 3 ½ inch micro floppy disk drive; no expansion slots; a keyboard with no function keys, numeric keypad or cursor control keys; a 16/32-bit Motorola 68000 microprocessor operating at a clock speed of 7.8336 MHz; a mouse used as a cursor control device; and a user-interface designed for 'the rest of us.' The initial list price for this 'toaster' of personal computers was $2495.00.

The most prominent feature of this system, however, was the user-interface and the mouse. The Mac employed an interface that has come to be known as a desktop environment. This typically employs overlapping windows, smaller sections of a screen containing output from parts of an application; icons, small graphic symbols representing various computer functions; and the mouse input device.

The Macintosh was not the first to employ this type of interface. For that you must go back to 1981 and the Xerox 8010 Star Information System, and to some extent even earlier to the experimental Xerox Alto computer in the late 1970s. This type of interface was later adopted by Niklaus Wirth in his Lilith project, and then released by Apple one year before the Macintosh with the Lisa. The Macintosh however, was the first machine to popularize this type of user interface.

The Mac, while being somewhat of a technological breakthrough, was not without its shortcomings. First, 128K of memory was nowhere near enough memory for significant business applications. 128K itself was actually a deceptive figure. With the amount of system overhead required to support the user interface, far less free memory was really available to the user. Another commonly cited fault was its lack of expansion capability. With no internal expansion slots and no provision for a second internal floppy disk drive the machine was short on flexibility. The lack of color display capability was another oft cited failing. Finally, the inability of the Macintosh to run MS-DOS kept the machine out of the mainstream of business application software.

Well, since 1984 the Mac has evolved quite a bit from the original 128K machine. The machine progressed over the years to the Fat Mac, Mac Plus, Macintosh SE, Macintosh II, various Power Macs and the latest incarnation, the iMac. Through this advancement all of the previously mentioned deficiencies have been redressed.

1984 saw the introduction of another major new machine as well, this time from IBM. By the fall of the year the IBM PC AT (for Advanced Technology) had hit the market. While not as technologically innovative as the Macintosh, the AT offered significant advancement of the standard IBM had established three years before.

The salient features of the AT included a true 16-bit Intel 80286 microprocessor operating at 6 MHz, a 1.2Mb high-density floppy disk drive, 256K of memory that was expandable to 3Mb and eight expansion slots. The basic machine listed for $3995.00.

The AT offered greater performance while still maintaining software compatibility with the existing MS-DOS software base. It also provided a platform for the next generation of software operating under OS/2.

In 1987, IBM released its PS/2 line of personal computers. To a large extent these differed quite a bit from the PC/XT/AT line of machines that preceded them.

The Personal System/2 computers sported 3½ - inch micro floppy drives, onboard graphics support and a modular assembly design. With the exception of the low-end Model 30, these machines boasted a new hardware bus called the Micro Channel, which, while not compatible with the older AT bus, offered instead high-speed data and I/O transfers, sharing resources and multi-processing support.

The Model 80 was the first IBM machine to make use of the 16MHz Intel 80386 32-bit microprocessor. This remained IBM's high-end machine until the 25 MHz Model 70 was introduced in 1988.

In addition to design differences from the PC/XT/AT line, IBM had decided to reduce some of the openness that had been associated with that line as well. For example, the ROM BIOS listing was not published, only the entry points were made available. As well, IBM, while documenting the electrical signals to the Micro Channel bus, patented the design.

The next chapter in this story brings back one of the pioneers in the field, Steve Jobs, formerly of Apple Computer. Jobs had been ousted as Chairman of Apple in 1985 as a result of a power struggle with his hand-picked choice for president, John Sculley, formerly of Pepsi. Upon his departure he took with him some of the best talent at Apple and set up a new company called NeXT, Inc.

After three years of work, seven million dollars of his own money and 20 million dollars in backing from H. Ross Perot, Jobs unveiled with great fanfare on October 12, 1988, the fruit of his labors, 'the cube.'

Received with mixed reviews by the industry, the machine was nonetheless certainly of technological significance. Termed 'the machine for the nineties' by Jobs, the stark, matte-black one-foot cube packed quite a punch. For $6500.00 you got a machine powered by a Motorola 68030 32-bit microprocessor running at 25 MHz, a 68882 math coprocessor, and 8Mb of RAM standard. The cube was connected to a 17-inch very high resolution monochrome monitor providing an excellent display. Mass storage on the machine was handled by a magneto-optical drive. The drive accepted 3 ½ - inch removable cartridges that hold 256Mb each. These drives operated on the same principal as compact disks utilizing laser technology. As well, the cube had a digital signal processing (DSP) chip enabling the machine to produce compact disk quality music in addition to sending and receiving voice mail.

NeXT ran a version of UNIX called Mach as the operating system. UNIX, a multi-user, multitasking operating system, was originally developed at Bell Labs in the early 1970s to run on large time-sharing systems. The rather user-unfriendly command syntax of UNIX was hidden by NeXT's windowing user interface called the Workspace Manager. The Workspace interface used a desktop metaphor like that on the Macintosh, however its implementation was not at all similar to the Mac.

There was also quite a bit of software bundled with NeXT's cube. In addition to the Mach operating system, the machine came with a C compiler, a text database, electronic mail, a word processor, a file manager, plus Webster's Dictionary and Thesaurus, the Oxford Dictionary of Quotations and the complete works of Shakespeare.

Despite its innovations, the NeXT cube never took-off. NeXT got out of the hardware business and the software side of the business was bought by Apple in the mid-90s.

Through most of the nineties, hardware continued to make significant advances with the IBM PC-compatibles effectively owning the business market. The graphical user interface offered by the Macintosh was emulated by the Microsoft Windows operating system. This basically eliminated any advantage that the Mac had over the IBM PC world. While the hardware advances were certainly impressive, with the current crop of PCs capable of running at a screaming 1 GHz, the real story of the '90s was Microsoft Windows.

While the first version of the Microsoft Windows operating environment was released back in 1985, the first truly useable version entered the scene in May of 1990. Released as version 3.0, this was the first successful attempt on the part of the Microsoft/Intel side of the computer world to really challenge the Macintosh head-on. Version 3.0 was a tremendous step-up from previous iterations and leaps and bounds beyond the c:\> of DOS. Nonetheless, it still couldn't compare to the tightly integrated graphical environment offered by the Macs. But Microsoft kept on trying. A couple of years later, in 1992, they submitted Windows version 3.1 which was a big improvement over version 3.0. Then in August of 1995, Microsoft finally rolled-out their long-anticipated new release, Windows 95. This was by far the most mature and effective version to date. And it actually gave the Mac folks a run for their money. The follow-up version of the operating system was called Windows 98. Released in June of 1998, this version added some polish to Windows 95, and integrated the operating system very tightly with the Internet. The most current iteration of the operating system is known as Windows ME (Millennium Edition). It is targeted primarily towards the consumer market.

Microsoft also developed a more business-oriented line of operating systems (OS) in parallel with those listed above. Known as Windows NT (for New Technology), this OS is primarily designed for computers linked together in a network environment. The most current version of NT, as of this writing, is Microsoft Windows 2000.

Computer Languages

Computer languages are the means by which the outside world communicates with the machine. The most basic of languages is, appropriately enough, machine language. Machine language requires the programmer to enter into the machine all of the instructions to be executed in binary 0s and 1s corresponding to the op codes (operation codes) of the microprocessor and the data to be operated upon. This was the only means of programming the earliest of computers. Needless to say, this was a tedious, time-consuming and error-prone means of controlling the machine.

To improve upon this obviously less than optimal situation symbolic languages were developed. Symbolic languages use mnemonics (memory aids) to facilitate program development. The most elementary of these is assembly language.

Assembly language offers a direct one-to-one relationship between mnemonic and microprocessor op code. The program that translates the mnemonics into machine-readable form is called an assembler. It is termed a low-level language due to the fact that the programmer must manipulate register contents and memory addresses to achieve his desired result.

Assembly language is not used as frequently as it had been several years ago. The main advantages of assembly language programs had been very high-speed operation and small size. Recently however, with the advent of mammoth memories, blindingly fast microprocessors and highly efficient optimizing compilers, these advantages no longer held the importance they once did. Those factors plus the greater level of difficulty in writing assembly code as opposed to high-level language code further diminished its appeal. Currently, assembly code is used for the most part for high speed procedures included within a larger high-level language application.

The following is a small 8086/88 assembly language program that prints 'hello, world' on the screen. As you can see, it isn't exactly the most intelligible thing to read, especially for those unfamiliar with programming in general. Assembly language is really the art and science of the most capable of programmers. Don't try this at home.

```
prognam segment
  assume cs:prognam
        mov dx,109
        mov ah,9
        int 21h
        int 20h
        db 'hello, world$'
    prognam ends
end
```

Our discussion now turns to high-level programming languages. These were first introduced in the mid-1950s to further simplify the programming process. There are two different methods of program translation of these high-level languages -- interpretation and compilation.

An interpreted language translates the humanly intelligible program language statements into machine intelligible machine language one at a time as the program executes. A compiled language reads the whole program and translates it in its entirety to machine language before it is run. In general, a compiled program will execute ten to twenty times faster than its interpreted counterpart. The advantage of an interpreted language had been that, due to its interactive nature, program development had been quicker than that for compiled languages. This is not quite the case any more though. Compilers in recent years have become so quick, and many are included with integrated editors, so that the advantage interpreters once had is no longer there.

The oldest high-level language is FORTRAN. 1957 saw the first programs compiled successfully in the language. The name is an acronym for FORmula TRANslator. Its initial use was for science, engineering and mathematics applications. Over the years the language definition has been extended so that other types of applications can be effectively written in it as well. Nonetheless, it is still used mainly for scientific problem solving.

The next major high-level language to be developed was COBOL. Like FORTRAN, COBOL is an acronym for COmmon Business Oriented Language. It was developed by a committee of business and government representatives specifically for writing business applications. The first COBOL compiler was introduced in 1959. The intent of the developers of COBOL was to create a language capable of handling any business application as well as using a syntax understandable to the non-programmer. Appropriately enough, a COBOL program consists of sentences and paragraphs for its structure. COBOL is still one of the most widely used programming languages. It never really caught on as a microcomputer development language though. Most COBOL compilers are installed on large mainframe or minicomputers.

Probably the most widespread high-level programming language installed on microcomputer systems today is BASIC. BASIC is an acronym for Beginners All-purpose Symbolic Instruction Code. John Kemeny and Thomas Kurtz developed it at Dartmouth College in 1964. As the name suggests, this language was intended as an easy to learn introduction to computer programming. It borrows quite a bit from FORTRAN. In its initial incarnation, BASIC was an interpreted language. This was also one of the factors that made it an easy language to learn and use. Over the years, BASIC has evolved into a much more powerful and flexible development language while still attempting to maintain its relative simplicity. Its latest versions are compiled rather than interpreted and offer many extensions that allow a true modular, structured style of programming.

In 1968, Niklaus Wirth invented Pascal (named in honor of French mathematician Blaise Pascal) as a hypothetical language to teach programming. By 1970 he had a working implementation of the language. Pascal has its roots in an earlier language called Algol. The initial purpose of Pascal was to teach the concepts of structured programming. Essentially, structured programming dictates that a program should be divided into numerous smaller sub-tasks -- procedures and functions -- each confined to performing a single task. The purpose of this is to simplify program development and maintenance, increase programmer productivity, reduce program complexity and encourage well-thought-out program design. Pascal has proliferated in academia, as one would expect from its original intent. As well, it has become a popular microcomputer development language. It is a powerful, full-featured language, and in its current implementations it can be used for writing almost any type of application.

The next major language to be covered in this discussion is C. Developed in 1972 at Bell Labs by Dennis Ritchie, C traces its heritage back to a language known as BCPL. From its inception, C has been closely associated with the UNIX operating system. This is largely due to the fact that UNIX is written, almost in its entirety, in C. However, there are compilers available for most major machines and operating systems. C is a general-purpose programming language that has been used with great success in writing operating systems, compilers and other 'systems-software.' It is a relatively low-level language and as such it has come to be used in many situations where assembly language was once the only feasible language. Many major commercial application software packages have been written in C as well. Currently, C is probably the leading microcomputer development language. Most good C compilers produce very fast code and development time is significantly less than it would be using assembly language. These factors and others virtually assure that C will be the language of choice for most serious microcomputer development work over the next several years.

In 1978, ten years after he developed Pascal, Niklaus Wirth defined its successor: Modula-2. By 1979, the compiler was complete. Developed to redress the shortcomings of Pascal, Modula-2 is certainly a success. Earlier Pascal compilers did not allow separate compilation of certain groupings of procedures and functions into reusable library units that could then be linked to and called by other programs. Pascal was also not very effective at dealing with things at the machine level. Modula-2 was designed to make up for these deficiencies. Modula-2 was from the start a systems programming language. In fact, it was designed to be the sole development language for Wirth's hardware project - Lilith - a windowing personal workstation alluded to previously. The most significant feature of Modula-2 as opposed to standard Pascal is the module concept. Reusable modules can drastically reduce program development time. A collection of thoroughly debugged, generic routines can be called by other programs and therefore not require the reinvention of the wheel with each new programming project. The advantages of Modula-2 over Pascal have diminished in the last couple of years or so though. Newer Pascal compilers have provided extensions to the language that offer most of the features of Modula-2 that were not originally part of Pascal. In any event, Modula-2 is a very versatile and powerful language.

Another newer language of some moment is C++ (pronounced C plus plus). C++ relates to C in much the same way that Modula-2 relates to Pascal. Implemented in 1983 by Bjarne Stroustrup of Bell Labs, C++ was originally created to develop simulation programs. C++, much like Modula-2, is a superset of its parent language, in this case - C. What differentiates C++ from C is that it implements the precepts of object-oriented programming.

Object-oriented programming takes the concepts of structured programming to their logical conclusion. The major building blocks of a program are called objects; these are protected areas of memory that can have both local variables and local procedures. There are generally two different types of objects, classes and instances. A class is a template on which each instance is modeled and provided with its own section of memory that cannot be accessed by any other object without using the object's own local methods. There are three major advantages to object-oriented programming. The first is that, once you have written the code for a class, you can have as many instances of that class present at one time, as memory will allow. Another advantage is that, through the mechanism of inheritance, subclasses automatically share all the variables and methods of their superclasses. The final advantage is an improved ability to handle complexity in a transparent manner.

In any event, C++ has been getting more and more popular among programmers as the object-oriented paradigm begins to catch on. It is certainly a worthy development language and a relatively easy one to migrate to from C.

The foregoing has certainly not been exhaustive list of programming languages. In fact, the languages mentioned do not even come close to covering all of the languages available to the developer. The ones we did cover, however, were the most significant in the evolution of computer languages and/or in use as microcomputer development languages.

Just so not to slight anyone's favorite language we can quickly list some other popular computer languages. In addition to what we previously covered there are languages called RPG, PL/1, APL, Forth, Ada, Lisp, Prolog, Actor, Smalltalk and the list goes on.

General Application Programs

A *computer program* is a detailed set of instructions telling a computer to do something. General application programs are the most common types of computer programs in use. Some people may disagree with this assessment, but to my way of thinking, there are three major categories of general application software. These are word processing, spreadsheet and database management. Most people who use a computer on a regular basis will have exposure to these types of programs.

Word processing programs allow the user to easily produce text documents. Because of their ease of use and powerful features, they have almost eliminated the need for typewriters. This work was completely prepared in a word processing program called *Microsoft Word*. *Word* is probably the most commonly used word processor on the market. Another popular offering is known as *Word Perfect*. In fact, *Word Perfect* had dominated the market for a number of years in the late '80s and early '90s. Word processors have a history dating back to almost as early as the release of the first mass-market microcomputers. The earliest word processor I can recall was something called *Electric Pencil*. In the early years, this market was dominated by an offering called *Word Star*.

Spreadsheet programs were probably responsible for launching the PC revolution in the business market. For the first time, up to that point, there was truly a valid use in a business environment for what had been largely a hobbyist's toy.

In 1979, Bob Frankston and Dan Bricklin invented the first spreadsheet, *VisiCalc*, for the Apple II and in so doing, put Apple on the corporate map. A spreadsheet is a grid of columns and rows on a computer screen, upon which a whole host of mathematical computations can be performed. The intersection of each column and row is called a *cell*. Columns are referenced by letters, while rows are referenced by numbers. Frankston and Bricklin formed a company called Software Arts and developed versions of *VisiCalc* for most of the major computer brands available on the market at the time. An example of what a spreadsheet looks like follows:

	A	B	C	D	E	F	G	H	I
1									
2	Origin:	Jersey City, NJ 07304	Class 55						
3			Zip		Weight		CF/Yellow	Titan '98	
4	State	City	Code		Breaks		Base Rates	Base Rates	% Difference
5									
6	AL	Birmingham	35209		500	$	184.10	$ 210.60	114.39%
7					1000	$	294.80	$ 343.60	116.55%
8					5000	$	951.50	$ 1,066.50	112.09%
9					10000	$	1,730.00	$ 1,871.00	108.15%
10					20000	$	3,460.00	$ 2,958.00	85.49%
11									
12		Mobile	36693		500	$	205.15	$ 233.00	113.58%
13					1000	$	328.50	$ 380.20	115.74%
14					5000	$	1,059.50	$ 1,180.50	111.42%
15					10000	$	1,928.00	$ 2,070.00	107.37%
16					20000	$	3,856.00	$ 3,272.00	84.85%
17									
18	AR	Little Rock	72209		500	$	204.10	$ 201.05	98.51%
19					1000	$	340.00	$ 335.80	98.76%
20					5000	$	1,191.50	$ 1,182.50	99.24%
21					10000	$	2,215.00	$ 2,117.00	95.58%
22					20000	$	4,430.00	$ 2,818.00	63.61%
23									
24	CT	Hartford	06101		500	$	131.55	$ 123.90	94.18%
25					1000	$	195.90	$ 181.10	92.45%
26					5000	$	625.50	$ 557.50	89.13%
27					10000	$	1,110.00	$ 954.00	85.95%
28					20000	$	2,220.00	$ 1,214.00	54.68%
29									
30	DE	Wilmington	19800		500	$	115.65	$ 131.70	113.88%
31					1000	$	182.80	$ 196.30	107.39%
32					5000	$	655.50	$ 595.50	90.85%
33					10000	$	1,161.00	$ 1,016.00	87.51%
34					20000	$	2,322.00	$ 1,238.00	53.32%

In 1982, an improved version of a spreadsheet was developed and marketed by a new company called Lotus Development. This new product, known as Lotus 1-2-3, combined the functionality of a spreadsheet, along with that of a simple data base and also some true graphics capabilities. The program was developed for the new IBM PC and it was a phenomenal success. Over the years, the spreadsheet model was expanded and refined through different offerings by different vendors. Programs such as *SuperCalc*, *Quattro Pro*, *Symphony*, and *Excel* have all added to the basic concept pioneered by *VisiCalc*. Overall, the spreadsheet is probably one of the most significant developments in the history of computer software. Because of the power and functionality afforded by this paradigm, the ability for financial analysts to perform complicated *what-if* analyses has become greatly facilitated. The spreadsheet is an accountant's dream come true.

Data base programs are the equivalent of an electronic filing cabinet. These powerful programs allow the user to store and retrieve massive amounts of information quickly and easily. They also allow for simple look-up, sorting and reporting of the stored data.

The are two primary types of data base programs - the *flat-file* data base and the *relational* data base. Before we get too in-depth here, it is time for some definitions.

A computer *file* is a collection of information, grouped and stored together, under a common name. For example, an employee name and address data base might be called *address.dat*. A data base file is comprised of groups of information known as *records*. Following the same address data base example, a record would consist of all the all the name and address information applicable to one person. Finally, each item in a data base record is called a *field*. So the last name of an employee would be considered one of the fields in a data base record. The total collection of data base records comprises the contents of the data base file. Here is how a data base record might be structured.

Last name: Jones	**First name:** William	**Middle initial:** A
Social security #: 123-45-6789		
Street address: 123 Main Street		
City: Jersey City	**State:** New Jersey	**Zip code:** 07304

Again, each piece of information, such as the last name, is called a field, the entire group of information for Mr. Jones is called a record, and the collective information on all the employees of an entire company would be the data base itself, stored in a file.

Getting back to our original train of thought, there are two different types of data bases - the flat-file and the relational data base. A flat-file data base stores all of its information in one file. Our simple example above is a flat-file data base. These are generally used where there are a limited number of fields in a record. In most cases, if the number of fields in a record exceed about 15 or so, then you will probably want to consider using a relational data base.

A relational data base stores larger amounts of related information across multiple files. These files are linked together by common fields known as *keys* or *indexes*. An employee data base would want to store more than just the information listed above. Such information as hire date, salary, marital status, etc., would need to be stored. Such additional information could be stored in a separate file called *employee.dat*. This may look something like this:

Social security #:	123-45-6789
Hire date: 01/01/1995	**Marital status:** Single
Annual salary: $35,000.00	

The key or index field is the social security number. When searching for information on Mr. Jones, the computer user would enter his social security number and the computer would respond with the information on Mr. Jones that is contained in both files. This is a complex concept and I hope it makes some sense to you based upon this very simplistic example.

The program that really established relational data bases in the PC world was called *dBase II*. dBase went through numerous improvements over the years, but was eventually replaced in general use by such offerings as *Paradox* or *Access*.

Other common general application programs you may encounter or be familiar with include graphics programs, presentation programs, project management programs and others.

Local Area Networks (LANs)

Local area networks (LANs) connect personal computers and various other equipment located within the confines of the same general geographic area, such as a floor of a building. They enable people to share equipment such as printers, fax machines, disk drives, as well as data and software. This connectivity allows for enhanced efficiencies and effectiveness of the people so connected.

Two of the most common applications for use on a network are sharing data bases and electronic mail (e-mail). Sharing a data base allows the users to view and operate on the same set of data while maintaining its accuracy and integrity for all users. E-mail enables those users connected to the LAN to communicate with each other electronically, and almost instantaneously, reducing paperwork and maintaining a history of all messages sent and received.

The method in which the individual components of a LAN are connected together is called its *topology*. There are three primary topologies used for connecting PCs and peripherals to a LAN: bus, star and ring.

The bus topology connects all the components on the LAN to a single, central cable. Expansion is easy and if one component fails to operate, it does not affect the rest of the LAN. The star topology connects all components through a central host computer. Adding components is easy, but if the host goes down, then the whole LAN ceases to function. The ring topology connects the components to one another in a circular layout.

The response time is quicker than that of a bus or star topology, but it is difficult to expand.

Electronic Data Interchange (EDI)

Electronic data interchange (EDI) is a means of electronically transmitting business data from one company's computer system to that of another company's. Typical uses for EDI are the transmission of purchase orders, invoices, bills of lading and freight bills. Its advantages are speed - it is almost instantaneous, accuracy and the reduction of paperwork.

EDI functions on the basis of a set of standards, allowing the data sent by one computer to be received and accurately interpreted by another. Both shippers and carriers enjoy the capabilities offered by EDI, and its acceptance as a medium for transmitting information is becoming more and more widespread.

The Internet

In 2001, no discussion of computers would be complete without mentioning the Internet. Over the past several years, the Internet and its graphical interface known as the World Wide Web have skyrocketed from relative obscurity to one of the fastest growing technologies to come along in years.

The Internet was originally developed by the U.S. Department of Defense in the 1970s as a computer network, which would be indestructible, even in the event of a nuclear attack. The Internet is designed in such a way that, even if one of the many participating servers becomes inoperable, the remainder of the network still functions. Its initial use was for governmental research and defense related activities.

While structurally the Internet is very nice, its usage remained quite limited until the introduction of the World Wide Web. The Web was developed at the European Particle Physics Lab as a means of easily sharing information about physics among the many physicists located around the world. The Web uses a standard method of representing data known as Hypertext Markup Language (HTML). The Web also uses a universal addressing system allowing for effortless access to every computer on the network.

Finally, what really enabled the rapid growth of the World Wide Web was a product called *Mosaic*. Developed in 1993 by University of Illinois student Marc Andreessen, *Mosaic* was the first graphical browser for the Web. *Mosaic* was available for free by downloading it from the University of Illinois' server. In the first two years since *Mosaic's* release, more than three million copies were downloaded or distributed through other means. In January 1993, when *Mosaic* was released, only 50 Web servers existed. By the end of 1995, that number had grown to over 100,000 servers.

In 1995, Andreessen and James Clark founded Netscape Corporation to market a product modeled on *Mosaic*. This improved browser, known as *Netscape Navigator*, grabbed 80% of the browser market within months of its release.

Since then, Netscape faced intense competition in this market from Microsoft and suffered tremendous market share erosion. Finally, in late 1998, Netscape was purchased by the country's largest on-line service, America Online.

Computers and Logistics

Well, I've just spent the last 20 pages or so describing some of the more technical aspects associated with personal computers. While it is not necessary to fully grasp all of this background material in order to take complete advantage of a PC in your operation, familiarity with some of it will help you understand a little better why things are the way they are. It can't hurt...

What I'd like to do now is spend some time looking at some specific uses for a PC in a logistics department. Obviously, there are the typical, general administrative chores that need to be done. And for these, the general application programs reviewed earlier fit the bill perfectly. Every department should have a PC available to them with a word processor, spreadsheet and data base installed on the hard drive. My advice to you: become completely competent in all of these. They are essential for making your department fully effective. Attend a seminar, take an adult school class or learn on your own, but please learn.

To me anyway, it seems rather obvious that one of the first things you should do with your PC is take advantage of some of the handy applications that your carriers are giving away. Almost every motor carrier will provide their rates to you on diskette. While they are all somewhat different in operation, they do provide the same functionality. With these programs you can quickly and accurately audit your freight bills and provide freight price quotations to your sales folks. The best part is they are free. They are very easy to use and quite handy.

If your PC gives you Internet access, you can access the Web sites of most major carriers and take advantage of a number of nice services. The small package carriers give you the ability to ship and track packages through their Web sites. Many of the major LTL carriers allow you to trace shipments through their Web sites as well.

Some of the major international freight forwarders allow you to directly connect with their large corporate mainframe computers through your PC. This enables you to have real-time information on the status of any of your international shipments and view a history of your shipments with that forwarder.

If possible, use EDI as part of your operation. Any opportunity to reduce or eliminate the amount of paper in your department is good. Most major carriers are set-up to use EDI as a normal part of doing business. Many carriers will even provide you with the software to transmit your bills of lading to them electronically.

If you export, be sure to purchase some type of export forms software. It will save you a ton of money over time and simplify the whole process. Instead of re-typing repetitive information over and over again on different forms, these programs allow you to enter data once, and then the software places it in the appropriate locations on the various forms. Once the data is entered, you can print out the forms you need for a particular shipment right on your own printer. These programs will often maintain a history of your export shipments too - quite a handy feature!

Of course, there are many other applications that are useful in a range of logistics departments, depending upon the industry to which you belong. For example, companies that ship mainly truckload volumes may have use for load-building programs or mileage calculation programs. There are programs to streamline the claims filing process. There are a multitude of programs to optimize freight routing from single or multiple plants.

As you can see by this brief discussion, the uses for a PC in the traffic department are vast. If you don't have one - beg, borrow or steal one. If you do have one - use it to its fullest extent.

Conclusion

This was one of the longer chapters in this work and probably the most challenging for many of you. I'm pretty sure that most readers of this book are familiar with computers to at least a limited degree. What I tried to accomplish was provide a brief explanation of some of the concepts a casual user would probably be either unfamiliar with, or need some additional background on to be truly computer literate. I hope I achieved my goal and you found the material of value.

Chapter 5

E-Logistics 101
or
What is all this e-stuff anyway?

With all the talk about the Internet and the World Wide Web over the past several years, it would be a glaring omission on my part to not take at least a summary look at how this phenomenon has affected logistics. In July of 2000, I participated in an e-logistics conference in Chicago, sponsored by the International Quality and Productivity Center. This chapter is an extract from my presentation.

How it all began

Before we begin our discussion of this topic, a few definitions are required. First things first, what the heck is the Internet? Well, the *Internet* is a computer network that links together computer systems all over the world by satellite and telephone, connecting users with service networks such as e-mail and the World Wide Web.

The Internet was originally launched way back in 1969. It was started as part of a Department of Defense initiative to design a computer network that would survive a nuclear attack even if one of the nodes (linked computers) was destroyed. Originally it consisted of four computers located across California and Utah.

Now how is that different from the World Wide Web? The World Wide Web (WWW) is a large set of linked documents and other files, located on computers connected through the Internet, that is used to access, manipulate and download data and programs. In other words, the Internet is the network and the Web is all the stuff on the network.

Tim Berners-Lee at the European Particle Physics Lab started the World Wide Web. Its original use was to share information about high-energy physics among physicists dispersed around the globe. The way they accomplished this was by developing a standard for representing data. This mechanism is known as Hypertext Markup Language

(HTML). The way it works is tags on a word or phrase can connect one computer to documents on the same computer or one across the world.

The real catalyst for launching the Web, as we know it today occurred back in 1993. University of Illinois student Marc Andreessen developed the first graphical browser for the Web in February of that year. It allowed users to view graphic images as well as text on the Web. He called his browser *Mosaic* and he offered it for free. Mosaic became the basis for Netscape Corporation and Mosaic evolved into Netscape Navigator.

The significance of the Web

Just how big is the Web? If you watch TV or read any newspapers or magazines, you would think that the Web is everywhere. You always see WWW this or .com that. Well, you are not too far off the mark.

To get a sense of the magnitude, I'd like to throw a few statistics at you. Bear in mind that with the exponential growth of the Web and the Internet, anything I tell you will be immediately outdated.

- Domain names (www.somesite.com) have increased from 26,000 in 1993 to 5,000,000 in 1999.
- Online usage in 1999 was estimated at 17.6 million total users.
- 760 U.S. households join the Internet every hour.
- There are seven new people on the Internet every second.
- Online retail sales exploded from $0.5 billion in 1995 to $7.8 billion in 1998.
- Online business-to-business sales will skyrocket from $45 billion in 1998 to an estimated $1.3 trillion in 2003.

Some pretty impressive numbers I would think and certainly something we in the logistics industry need to recognize.

The New Economy

The Internet has definitely affected the way business is transacted. In fact, as a consequence of its impact, we have something known as the New Economy. The New Economy primarily refers to doing business via the Internet. Some of the key principles of the new economy are:

- It is more oriented towards information rather than things.
  - Information is one of the key commodities as we begin the new millennium.
- It realizes and capitalizes on the power of the network.
  - As a network grows its value increases exponentially.
- It understands the value of giving things away.
  - How many Web sites make money by giving their products away? Their revenue stream comes from growth in their communities and through advertising revenue.
- Plentitude, not scarcity, are the key to wealth and value.

- The old economy is based on supply and demand. The less some thing is available, the more people will be willing to pay a premium for it. The New Economy flourishes through the growth of the network. The more users, members, eyeballs, etc., the greater the revenue.

Business 2.0 magazine, an excellent New Economy magazine, published a series of articles listing what it believed to be the 10 driving principles of the New Economy. I have seen a number of articles similar to these, but I like theirs best. They are listed below and are essentially self-explanatory.

1. **Matter**. It matters less.
2. **Space**. Distance has vanished.
3. **Time**. It's collapsing.
4. **People**. They are your most important asset and they know it.
5. **Growth**. It is accelerated by the network.
6. **Value**. It rises exponentially with market share.
7. **Efficiency**. The middleman lives.
8. **Markets**. Buyers are gaining dramatic new power and sellers new opportunities.
9. **Transactions**. It's a one-on-one game.
10. **Impulse**. Every product is available everywhere.

Impact of the Internet on Logistics

There are several primary benefits for logistics by leveraging the Internet. Most significant among them are:

- Speed
- Reduced Cost
- Operational Efficiencies
- Improved Information Flow
- Improved Customer Service

So, as logistics practitioners, how do we take advantage of these benefits? Well, let's see what some Web sites have to offer us and find out.

Every major carrier and freight forwarder has a Web site and most of them have some pretty decent functionality. The days of just having a brochure site are done. Some of the more common features that these sites may offer are:

- Real-time tracking and tracing
- Booking pick-ups on-line
- Bill of lading/delivery receipt document imaging and printing
- Shipping assistance
- Create export documents on-line
- Access company specific pricing and discounts

Another potential use for the Internet is to auction your freight on-line. There are many companies that will let you submit a shipment and have several providers bid on moving it. You can then review the quotes and select the carrier you prefer. There are companies that do this for trucking, airfreight, ocean freight, small-package express freight, etc.

Some of the better sites are:

- GoCargo.com - Ocean freight
- Celarix.com - Ocean freight
- Freightquote.com - trucking
- iShip.com - small-package

As well, there are on-line purchasing communities that allow companies within specific commodity groups to efficiently trade with one another and perhaps enjoy the benefits of some economies of scale. Two of these are:

- MetalSite.com
- E-Chemicals.com

Application Service Providers (ASPs)

A new type of software vendor is making great headway in the application software community. These companies are known as ASPs or application service providers. Essentially what they do is offer to their customers "rented" software over a network (Internet) using pay-as-you-go pricing. In other words, you pay a monthly fee to use their software. These companies specifically target small- to mid-size companies that generally would not have the resources to purchase this software outright. The benefit is that you have at your disposal complicated software programs without the cost of installation, hardware or software. The software is accessed via the Internet.

Thee advantages are:

- Sophisticated software for a monthly fee.
- Reduced technology complexity.
- Reduced risk by eliminating the economic burden of buying hardware and software.
- Applications become universally available, affordable and easy to deploy.

As with anything though, there are some potential downsides. These include:

- No equity
- Very little control
- Severe consequences for early exit from a contract

Three logistics ASPs are Celarix.com, logistics.com and ShipLogix.com. This is a quite new business model and consequently, there are not many very mature players. It is a concept worth considering but be wary. Check references very carefully before you jump on the bandwagon.

Logistics Directories

Finally, there are a group of sites that specialize in logistics information. These are known as directory or portal sites. They offer to the logistics professional a means of contacting other logistics providers, conducting discussions with other members of the field, job search facilities, and a host of other services. Some of the nicer sites in this segment of the market are:

- LogisticsWorld.com
- About.com logistics
- LogisticsZone.com
- Logisticsnetwork.com (my own site)

Conclusion

That wraps up my very brief look at e-logistics. Granted it is only a taste, but I hope it gives you a flavor for what is available and serves as a spur to investigate further on your own. Happy surfing!

Appendix A

Recommended Reading & Selected Bibliography

Logistics Specific

Ackerman, K.B. (1986). Practical Handbook of Warehousing. Washington, D.C.: The Traffic Service Corporation.

Augello, W.A. (1994). Doing Business Under the New Transportation Law: The Negotiated Rates Act of 1993. Huntington, NY: Transportation Claims and Prevention Council.

Augello, W.A. (1996). A Guide to Transportation After the Sunsetting of the ICC. Huntington, NY: Transportation Claims and Prevention Council.

Barrett, C. (1987). Practical Handbook of Computerization for Distribution managers. Washington, D.C.: The Traffic Service Corporation.

Blanding, W. (1982). Blanding's Practical Physical Distribution. Washington, D.C.: The Traffic Service Corporation.

Dobler, D.W., Lee, L. Burt, D.N. (1984). Purchasing and Materials Management. New York: McGraw-Hill.

Fearon, H.E., Dobler, D.W., Killen, K.H. (1993). The Purchasing Handbook. New York: McGraw-Hill.

The Global Logistics Research Team at Michigan State University. (1995). World Class Logistics: The Challenge of Managing Continuous Change. Oak Brook, IL: Council of Logistics Management.

Johnson, T.E. (1997). Export/Import Procedures and Documentation. New York: AMACOM.

Morse, L.W. (1980). Practical Handbook of Industrial Traffic Management. Washington, D.C.: The Traffic Service Corporation.

Nelson, R.A. (1985). Computerizing Warehouse Operations. Englewood Cliffs, NJ: Prentice-Hall.

Ovens, E.A. (1978). Transportation and Traffic Management, Vol. I. Washington, D.C.: The Traffic Service Corporation.

Ovens, E.A. (1979). Transportation and Traffic Management, Vol. II. Washington, D.C.: The Traffic Service Corporation.

Ovens, E.A. (1980). Transportation and Traffic Management, Vol. III. Washington, D.C.: The Traffic Service Corporation.

Ovens, E.A. (1979). Transportation and Traffic Management, Vol. IV. Washington, D.C.: The Traffic Service Corporation.

Ramberg, J. (1999). ICC Guide to Incoterms 2000. New York: ICC Publishing, Inc.

Reynolds, F. (1996). Export Documentation, Procedures and Terms of Sale. New Providence, NJ: Unz & Co., Inc.

Reynolds, F. (1999). Incoterms for Americans. Toledo, OH: International Projects, Inc.

Southern, R.N. (1997). Transportation and Logistics Basics. Memphis, TN: Continental Traffic Service, Inc.

U.S. Department of Commerce. (1998). A Basic Guide to Exporting. Washington, D.C.: Unz & Company.

General Business

Alter, S. (1996). Information Systems. Menlo Park, CA: The Benjamin/Cummings Publishing Company, Inc.

Bohl, M. (1980). Information Processing. Chicago: SRA, Inc.

Downes, L. & Mui, C. (1998). <u>Unleashing the Killer App: Digital Strategies for Market Dominance.</u> Boston: Harvard Business School Press.

Kelly, K. (1998). <u>New Rules for the New Economy: 10 Radical Strategies for a Connected World.</u> New York: Viking Penguin.

Mougayar, W. (1998). <u>Opening Digital Markets: Battle Plans and Business Strategies for Internet Commerce.</u> New York: McGraw-Hill.

Schaffer, R., Earle, B. & Agusti, F. (1996). <u>International Business Law and its Environment.</u> St. Paul, MN: West Publishing Company.

Tapscott, D. (1996). <u>The Digital Economy.</u> New York: McGraw-Hill.

Appendix B

Educational Institutions

Below is a partial listing of some of the better known college-level logistics programs in the United States. Some schools offer only undergraduate degrees, while others offer programs at a doctoral level.

College or University	Location	Phone	Degree Programs
Michigan State University	East Lansing, MI	517-355-2177	BS, MS, Ph. D.
Northwestern University	Evanston, IL	847-491-2276	MS, Ph. D.
Ohio State University	Columbus, OH	614-292-2329	BS, MS, Ph. D.
Penn State University	University Park, PA	814-865-1866	BS, MS, Ph. D.
St. John's University	Staten Island, NY	718-390-4494	BS
Syracuse University	Syracuse, NY	315-443-3442	BS, MBA, Ph. D.
The Logistics Institute - Georgia Institute of Technology	Atlanta, GA	404-894-2343	EMIL
Thomas Edison State College	Trenton, NJ	609-984-1150	ASM, BSBA
University of Tennessee	Knoxville, TN	423-974-5001	BS, MS, Ph. D.
University of Wisconsin - Madison	Madison, WI	608-262-1941	MS, MBA

Appendix C

Transportation & Logistics Organizations

Below is a partial listing of some of the more significant organizations dedicated to the transportation and logistics professional.

American Society of Transportation & Logistics (AST&L), 229 Peachtree Street, Suite 401, Atlanta, GA 30303

American Trucking Association (ATA), 2200 Mill Road, Alexandria, VA 22314

Council of Logistics Management (CLM), 2803 Butterfield, Suite 380, Oak Brook, IL 60521

Delta Nu Alpha Transportation Fraternity (DNA), 530 Church Street, Suite 300, Nashville, TN 37219

National Industrial Transportation League (NITL), 1700 North Moore Street, Suite 900, Alexandria, VA 22209

National Small Shipments Traffic Conference (NASSTRAC), Pennsylvania Avenue NW, Suite 1111, Washington, DC 20006

Society of Logistics Engineers (SOLE), 8100 Professional Place, Suite 211, Hyattsville, MD 20785

Transportation Consumer Protection Council (TCPC), 120 Main Street, Huntington, NY 11743

Warehousing Education & Research Council (WERC), 1100 Jorie Boulevard, Suite 170, Oak Brook, IL 60521

Appendix D

Useful Web Sites

Below is a partial listing of some useful Web sites for the transportation and logistics professional.

Site Name	Uniform Resource Locator (URL)
ABF Freight System	www.abfs.com
American Society of Transportation & Logistics	www.astl.org
Bureau of Export Administration	www.bxa.doc.gov
CIA World Factbook	www.odci.gov/cia/publications/nsolo.w fb-help/index.htm
Consolidated Freightways	www.cfwy.com
Council of Logistics Management	www.clm1.org
Federal Express	www.fedex.com
FedEx Ground	www.fedex.com/us/ground/
Federation of International Trade Associations	www.fita.org
International Business Magazine	www.internationalbusiness.com
International Calling Codes	www.the-acr.com/codes/cntrycd.htm
International Society of Logistics	www.sole.org
International Trade Law	itl.irv.uit.no/trade_law
Journal of Commerce	www.joc.com
logisticsnetwork.com	www.logisticsnetwork.com
Roadway Express	www.roadway.com
Trade Compass	www.tradecompass.com
Transportation Research Tools	www.fuld.com/i3/l47.html
U.S. International Trade Administration	www.ita.doc.gov/
United Parcel Service (UPS)	www.ups.com
Wall Street Journal	www.wsj.com

World Bank	www.worldbank.org/html/extdr/country.htm
World Trade Magazine	www.worldtrademag.com
Yellow Freight	www.yellowfreight.com

Appendix E

Please complete this form and fax it to {*insert your name here*}, {*insert your title here*}, {*insert company name here*} **at (999) 555-5555 or detach this form and e-mail confirmation to** your-email@your-company.com **at receipt of this package. Acknowledgment is due no later than** {*date & time*}.

LETTER OF RECEIPT

This letter acknowledges that _____
Company Name) has received and opened the request for proposal package from {*insert company name here*} dated {*date*}.

Date:

Signature:

Print Name:

Title:

{date}

Dear Valued Supplier,

Please find following a Request for Proposal (RFP) authored by {insert company name here}. We welcome any and all input you may provide us toward achievement of our goal of reducing {insert company name here} total cost of logistics and freight movement.

Our objective is to understand the full portfolio of services and options that you offer and to match supplier capabilities with corporate requirements.

The enclosed RFP is due back to {insert company name here} **absolutely no later** than *{date and time}* at the address below:

> {insert your name and address here}

Hard copies of proposal responses are also due to *{insert your name here}, {due date}*.

{insert company name here} has been working on initiatives aimed at reducing internal costs as well as costs of purchased goods and services. We have been tasked with reviewing the company's freight spend and developing and implementing ideas to reduce this spend. This RFP is designed to allow you to creatively demonstrate your capabilities and competencies in this important area of our business.

Any questions or other inquiries from your company concerning the RFP should be submitted in writing via electronic mail to *{insert your name here}*, your-email@your-company.com.

Sincerely,

{insert your name here}

CONFIDENTIAL

GLOBAL FREIGHT FORWARDING RFP

{INSERT COMPANY NAME HERE}

{insert date here}

TABLE OF CONTENTS

RFP Component

I. OVERVIEW OF RFP PROCESS

Background

{insert company name here} is currently undertaking a series of actions to improve operating performance. One major initiative underway is a broad effort to review *{insert company name here}* procurement of various products and services. Freight expenses are a major component of that spend and, therefore, a primary focus of this effort. *{insert company name here}* annual Global Freight Forwarder spend (all modes) is in excess of *{insert amount $$}*. *{insert company name here}* objectives for this effort are to reduce "total cost of ownership" for freight movements by *{amount %}* in the first year of engagement with continual additional savings of *{amount %}* per year. We will ask you to specifically indicate an annual cost savings/productivity improvement number in your proposal and outline your process for identification of opportunities and project management approach toward those savings. It is our intent to hold quarterly meetings with the successful supplier(s) in order to monitor progress and report achievements.

This RFP is an invitation for you to participate in our competitive proposal process. It is being distributed to existing and potential new suppliers.   Suppliers' responses to this RFP and our discussions with them will be used to select one or more suppliers to serve *{insert company name here}* Global Freight Forwarding and logistics needs.

{insert company name here} is prepared to take steps necessary to achieve our objective, including working with existing suppliers, or if appropriate, awarding business to new suppliers based on their ability to provide quality services at competitive prices.

Scope and Objectives of RFP

{insert company name here} is requesting proposals for competitive prices and cost savings across the gamut of inbound and outbound freight spend. We encourage suppliers to be creative, as we are open to any and all suggestions at this point. We also encourage you to provide multiple options, if desired. It is to your advantage to propose multiple options as we may rule out certain approaches as the process moves forward.

The RFP is designed to help *{insert company name here}* quickly determine which types of options, and which carriers, have the highest potential. Subsequent to the RFP, *{insert company name here}* will conduct a series of detailed negotiations with selected suppliers to determine the optimal supplier mix.

Criteria for Supplier Selection

{*insert company name here*} primary objective is to move freight within reasonable service guidelines at the lowest total cost of ownership. In determining which proposal(s) will best serve the interests of {*insert company name here*}, Suppliers will be evaluated based on their ability to provide:

- The lowest total cost to {*insert company name here*} based upon quoted rates;

- Broad global network of company owned offices;

- Significant IT capabilities which would be available to {insert company name here};

- Demonstrated 3PL/4PL global capabilities;

- Consistently high service quality across all shipments and locations;

- An explicit commitment (i.e. agreed-upon improvement targets) for continuous improvements in total cost;

- Detailed implementation plans to assist us in any efforts that may be required to transition to new suppliers;

- Detailed implementation plans for any suggested cost savings programs;

- Consistent execution of the agreed upon contract.

These objectives should be kept in mind as you formulate your response.

RFP Process

RFP Process Overview

Instructions for the RFP are included with the relevant section. You should fill out all information requested and use the enclosed checklist to confirm that you have included all relevant data.

Additionally, please pay special attention to the Qualitative Questions Section if you are proposing additional options for {*insert company name here*} that are not conducive to the rate matrices provided. The summaries submitted as a part of that section will be particularly helpful in allowing the team to evaluate the proposals in an expeditious manner.

RFP Contact Information

{*insert name and address here*}

RFP Questions, Inquiries, and Clarifications

Any questions or other inquiries from your company concerning this RFP must be submitted in writing or via electronic mail to {*insert your name here*}. (e-mail: your-name@your-company.com). Inquiries regarding the data in the Lane/Volume Matrix must be addressed in writing to the appropriate contact's email as noted in the Matrix body. All written questions/inquiries regarding clarification of the RFP will be answered in writing or via electronic mail and sent to all companies that are participating in this RFP. You must submit such questions in writing. **Questions will be accepted through {*insert date and time here*}. Answers will be mailed by {*insert due date*}. No questions will be taken after the {*insert due date*} deadline. All other communication must also be directed to {*insert company name here*} designated contacts.**

Proposal Format

Your proposal must be prepared simply and economically in strict accordance with the format and instructional requirements of this RFP. Your proposal should provide a concise delineation of your company's capabilities to satisfy the requirements of this RFP, with emphasis on completeness and clarity of content. **Elaborate bindings, displays, and promotional material are neither required nor desired unless they add substance to your company's proposal.** INCOMPLETE PROPOSALS OR PROPOSALS THAT ARE NOT PREPARED IN ACCORDANCE WITH THIS RFP WILL BE ELIMINATED FROM THE EVALUATION PROCESS. All companies are required to present proposals using the same headings and categories as outlined in the RFP to ensure a fair, equitable, and timely evaluation. {*insert company name here*} reserves the right to reject any and all proposals submitted that fail to conform to the requirements of the RFP and to request additional information from any company submitting a proposal.

Proposal Submittal Guidelines

Please prepare {*insert number*} hard copies of your proposal response and distribute directly to each team member as noted in the Contact Directory in the RFP appendix. An electronic version of your proposal must also be submitted to {*insert name*} at the email address listed above. The returned responses must be formatted identically to the originally distributed RFP.

Responses to this RFP must be delivered to the {*insert company name here*} team on or before {*date and time*}. Extensions will not be granted; early submittals are encouraged. The proposal must be complete in all aspects and may be rejected if conditional or incomplete. An Officer, Director, or Agent of the respondent who is legally authorized by the respondent to enter into a binding contract must sign the proposal, agreeing to the Terms and Conditions.

Proposal Interview/Supplier Meeting RFP Component

Upon successful submission, receipt, and review of your RFP you may be requested to present additional collateral at a personal interview. These interview meetings will be held at {*insert company name and address here*} on {*insert date*}. You will be advised as to specific date and time of expected presentation.

Supplemental Information

Unless supplemental oral commentary is specifically requested by {*insert company name here*}, oral communications outside the scope of the procedures detailed in this RFP will not be considered in connection with any company's proposal. *Should {insert company name here}* elect to award a contract to your company, your proposal and any supplemental information and responses will be incorporated into and made a part of any final agreement between {*insert company name here*} and your company. No such information or other material should be submitted that cannot be so incorporated into the agreement.

Modification of Request for Proposal

After {*insert company name here*} analysis of proposals submitted in response to this RFP, {*insert company name here*} may elect to modify the requirements of this RFP; {*insert company name here*} may also request resubmission from some or all of the selected participants.

Proposal Validity

Your proposal shall be assumed to remain valid for a period of 120 days after the proposal submittal deadline set forth above, unless you clearly indicate otherwise.

RFP Terms, Conditions, and Disclaimers

{*insert company name here*} has issued this RFP to solicit proposals from potential freight and logistics suppliers for a comprehensive solution to the requirements as outlined in this document. This document contains information and instructions for the preparation of a Proposal that will enable you to address the technical, financial, and legal requirements necessary. **It is not an offer to contract.** Only the execution of a written contract will obligate {*insert company name here*} in accordance with the terms and conditions contained in such contract

All costs associated with the preparation of a Proposal or contract in response to this RFP will be borne solely by the supplier. {*insert company name here*} will not reimburse your company for any proposal preparation costs or other work performed in connection with this RFP, whether or not your company is awarded a contract.

All Proposals shall become the property of {*insert company name here*}.

{insert company name here} **may enter into negotiations with more than one supplier simultaneously and award the transaction to any supplier in negotiations without prior notification to any other supplier currently negotiating with** *{insert company name here}*.

For purposes of the evaluation process, *{insert company name here}* reserves the right to make copies of your Proposal.

{insert company name here} reserves the right to verify all information provided by a supplier via direct contact with the supplier's clients and prior personnel, and the supplier must agree to provide and release necessary authorizations for *{insert company name here}* to verify any of the supplier's previous work. Supplier should inform references that a *{insert company name here}* representative might be contacting them. Misstatements of experience and scope of prior work may be grounds for disqualification of the supplier.

Please be advised that *{insert company name here}* is not committed to any course of action as a result of its issuance of this RFP and/or its receipt of a proposal from you or other companies in response to it. In particular, you should note that *{insert company name here}* may:

- Reject any proposal not conforming to instructions and specifications

- Not accept proposals after the stated submission deadline

- Not necessarily accept the lowest priced proposal

- Reject all proposals, if it so decides

- Negotiate with one or more companies

- Award a contract in connection with this RFP at any time

- Award only a portion of the contract

- Exclude from the contract any site outside of supplier's reasonable service range

- Make no award of a contract

Confidentiality

{insert company name here} **will not disclose or share one supplier's response to this RFP with another competing supplier or other organization,** but it shall be permitted to share the responses with *{insert company name here}* employees or with contract professionals working with *{insert company name here}* on this project.

All information received by supplier in connection with this RFP is the confidential information of *{insert company name here}*. Supplier may not use, disclose, or duplicate this RFP for any purpose other than preparing a response as requested in this document without obtaining *{insert company name here}* prior written consent. Supplier shall keep *{insert company name here}* data confidential and prevent its disclosure to any other party. Further, supplier shall restrict the disclosure of this RFP and {*insert company name here*} data to those of supplier's employees who have a need to know.

II. OVERVIEW OF {INSERT COMPANY NAME HERE}

Information regarding {*insert company name here*} global businesses may be viewed at the following websites:

www.your-company.com

III. *{insert company name here}* Expectations of Global Freight Forwarders

Delivery and Pick-up

- 100% on time delivery
- 100% on time pick-up
- Ability to accommodate specific *{insert company name here}* Company customers unique delivery requirements Weekend pick-ups a plus
- Ability to pick-up and deliver with-in locations' times of operation

Quality

- Claims ratio less than 4 per thousand shipments.
- Percentage of correct billings to total number of billings not less than 99 percent
- Established quality program (ISO 9000, QS 9000, or internal program)

Information systems

- Electronic billing (EDI)
- Satellite tracking
- E-mail capability
- Shipment data feedback via EDI or Internet
- Internet shipment tracking, claim filing, etc.
- Advanced/customized report formats
- Company to Company electronic interface design
- Web enabled Export Documentation system
- Online shipment booking

Equipment

- Access to high-quality and safe equipment
- Ability to spot containers for continuous loading

Administration

- Dispatcher available for shipment coordination with suppliers
- 24-hour dispatch and contact phone number
- Designated *{insert company name here}* Global account representative; other sector or geographic structure as defined

- Monthly service reports must be made available on a corporate basis as well as division, sector, and plant level and will include:
  - Inbound on-time delivery percentage
  - Outbound on-time delivery percentage
  - Continuous improvement activity
  - Missed shipment corrective action report
  - Claims ratio and status of outstanding claims
- Credit terms are to be negotiated at RFP submission
- Ability to provide customized load documentation per {insert company name here} Company requirements.

Attitude

- Carrier must demonstrate:
  - a customer led attitude (flexibility and focus on needs of {*insert company name here*})
  - a commitment to continuous improvement
  - a desire to develop a relationship with {*insert company name here*} Company top management

Continuous Improvement

- Resources made available upon request for cross-functional improvement activities
- Semi-annual meeting to review business plan

IV. INSTRUCTIONS FOR RFP PROCESS

Please submit the following items:

- Rate matrix

- Executive Summary of Options Proposed

- Annual cost savings/productivity improvement numbers and monitoring process overview

- Responses to the carrier qualitative questions

- A copy of your most recent Global Office Directory

- Explanation of current Information Technology, including but not limited to: EDI billing, internet tracing systems, web enabled Export Document preparation and shipment booking (or plans to implement such systems)

- List of local representatives for each major {*insert company name here*} site

V. Qualitative Questions

Please answer this entire set of questions. These questions center on a supplier's background/experience, pricing strategy, delivery/responsiveness and technology services.

Specific information about your company and capabilities is a critical part of our analysis. Please respond directly and thoroughly to **all** questions listed below.

A. Continuous Improvement

As a part of our effort, we are looking for suppliers who support relationships where there is a joint effort made toward reducing the total cost of freight shipments. These efforts should be to the mutual benefit of our suppliers and {*insert company name here*}. As such, we will look favorably upon suppliers who can commit to assisting {*insert company name here*} in our ongoing efforts of maintaining the lowest total cost of moving freight. It is within this context that we ask the following questions:

– What kinds of continuous improvement initiatives will you commit to?

– What kinds of targets will you set?

– How will performance against these commitments be measured, and how do we ensure that we share in the successes?

B. Value-Added services

1. Please outline any value-added services (with costs, where applicable) that you offer and feel could be of value to {*insert company name here*}.

C. Changes in the organization

Are there any major changes (acquisitions, restructuring, alliances, union negotiations, or joint ventures) taking place in your organization that could impact how you would serve {*insert company name here*} needs?

D. Technology

1. What systems do you use to support your freight movements?

2. Do you provide web enabled tracing, export documentation, shipment booking, report generation tools on-line?

E. Additional Proposals

Do you have any additional proposals not accounted for in the RFP provided? If so, what are they? What cost savings might they achieve?

(You may include a 1-2 page executive summary, if appropriate, for each additional proposal offered).

VI. Rate Matrix

Please refer to the Specific Lane Matrix attached to the introductory email:

{insert file name here}

The matrix contains *{insert number}* worksheets:

> *{insert worksheet names}*

Please fully and accurate complete each line item.

Inquiries to specific items contained within the Matrix are to be addressed in writing via email, per instructions included in the Matrix, to the appropriate *{insert company name here}* representative.

Accessorial Fees/ Exceptions Page

APPENDIX:

TIMELINE FOR PROCESS

Activity	Date(s)
RFP Package Sent Out	*{insert due date}*
Due Date for Letter of Receipt of RFP	*{insert due date}* *{insert time}*
Deadline for responses from Suppliers	*{insert due date}* *{insert time}*
Meetings with Suppliers at {insert location here}	*{insert dates}* Schedule TBD
First communication with Suppliers; RFP assessment progress	*{insert due date}* *{insert time}*
RFP Award(s) communicated	*{insert due date}* *{insert time}*

APPENDIX:

RFP CHECKLIST

_____ Rate matrix

_____ Executive summary of options proposed

_____ Annual cost savings/productivity improvement numbers and monitoring process overview

_____ Responses to carrier qualitative questions

_____ Global Office Directory

_____ Explanation of Information Technology Tools and Capabilities

_____ List of local representatives for each major {_INSERT COMPANY NAME HERE_} site

APPENDIX:

Contacts

Appendix F

On the following pages, you will find dimensions and graphics of some of the more common types of ocean and airfreight cargo containers. And in addition, we have included some standard truck dimensions as well.

CONTAINERS

20 FT. CONTAINER, OPEN TOP

INSIDE DIMENSIONS

LENGTH: 5,890 m 19'4"
WIDTH: 2,320 m 7'7 1/4"
HEIGHT: 2,150 m 7'0 9/16"

INTERNAL CUBIC CAPACITY

29,2 CBM 1030 cubic feet

MAX GROSS CAPACITY

18,110 kg 39,925 pounds

TARE WEIGHT (UNLADEN WEIGHT)

2,210 kg 4,872 pounds

OUTSIDE DIMENSIONS

LENGTH: 6,055 m 19'10 1/2"
HEIGHT: 2,428 m 8'0"
WIDTH: 2,438 m 8'0"

20 FT. PLATFORM

INSIDE DIMENSIONS

LENGTH: MAX. 5,919 m 19'7 7/8"
          MIN. 5,907 m 19'4 3/8"
HEIGHT: MAX. 2,260 m 7'5"
          MIN. 2,232 m 7'3 7/8"
WIDTH: MAX. 2,349 m 7'8 1/2"
          MIN. 2,331 , 7'7 3/4"

INTERNAL CUBIC CAPACITY

MAX. 31,5 CBM 1113 cubic feet
MIN. 30,8 CBM 1087 cubic feet

MAX GROSS CAPACITY

MAX. 18,670 kg 41,160 pounds
MIN. 18,460 kg 40,704 pounds

DOOR OPENING

HEIGHT: MAX. 2,159 m 7'1"
          MIN. 2,130 m 6'11 7/8"
WIDTH: MAX. 2,349 m 7'8 1/2"
          MIN. 2,247 m 7'4 7/16"

TARE WEIGHT (UNLADEN WEIGHT)

MAX. 1,860 kg 4,101 pounds
MIN. 1,650 kg 3,640 pounds

OUTSIDE DIMENSIONS

LENGTH: 6,055 m 19'10 1/2"
HEIGHT: 2,438 m 8'0"
WIDTH: 2,438 m 8'0"

CONTAINERS

40 FT. CONTAINER, HALFWAY, OPEN TOP

INSIDE DIMENSIONS

LENGTH: MAX. 12,065 m 39'7"
MIN. 12,063 m 39' 6 15/16"
HEIGHT: MAX. 1,059 m 3'6"
MIN. 0,935 m 3'0 13/16"
WIDTH: MAX. 2,354 m 7'8 11/16"
MIN. 2,340 m 7'8"

INTERNAL CUBIC CAPACITY

MAX. 26,510 kg 58,450 pounds
MIN. 26,130 kg 57,606 pounds

DOOR OPENING

HEIGHT MAX. 2,254 m 7'4 3/4"
MIN. 1,997 m 6'6 5/8"
WIDTH MAX. 2,350 m 7'8 1/2"
MIN. 2,118 m 6'11 3/8"

TARE WEIGHT (UNLADEN WEIGHT)

MAX. 4,350 kg 9,590 pounds
MIN. 3,790 kg 8,750 pounds

OUTSIDE DIMENSIONS

LENGTH: 12,190 m 40'0"
HEIGHT: MAX. 2,590 m 8'6"
MIN. 2,438 m 8'0"
WIDTH: 2,438 m 8'0"

40 FT. DRY CARGO CONTAINER

INSIDE DIMENSIONS

LENGTH: MAX. 12,065 m 39'7"
MIN. 12,025 m 39'5 3/8"
HEIGHT: MAX. 2,397 m 7'10 3/8"
MIN. 2,230 m 7'3 13/16"
WIDTH: MAX. 2,349 m 7'8 1/2"
MIN. 2,329 m 7'7 3/4"

INTERNAL CUBIC CAPACITY

MAX. 68,0 CBM 2401 cubic feet
MIN. 63,2 CBM 2232 cubic feet

DOOR OPENING

HEIGHT: MAX. 2,290 m 7'6 5/32"
MIN. 2,130 m 6'11 7/8"
WIDTH: MAX. 2,349 m 7'8 1/2"
MIN. 2,259 m 7'5"

TARE WEIGHT (UNLADEN WEIGHT)

MAX: 3,875 kg 8,542 pounds
MIN. 2,745 kg 6,040 pounds

OUTSIDE DIMENSIONS

LENGTH: 12,190 m 40'0"
HEIGHT: MAX. 2,590 m 8'6"
MIN. 2,438 m 8'0"
WIDTH: 2,438 m 8'0"

CONTAINERS

40 FT. CONTAINER, OPEN TOP

INSIDE DIMENSIONS

LENGTH:	MAX. 12,070 m 39'7"
	MIN. 12,015 m 39'5"
HEIGHT:	MAX. 2,301 m 7' 6 5/8"
	MIN. 2,102 m 6'10 3/4"
WIDTH:	MAX. 2,354 m 7'8 11/16"
	MIN. 2,332 m 7'7 3/4"

INTERNAL CUBIC CAPACITY

MAX. 65.0 CBM 2295 cubic feet
MIN. 58,9 CBM 2082 cubic feet

MAX GROSS CAPACITY

MAX. 26,510 kg. 58,450 pounds
MIN. 26,130 kg. 57,606 pounds

DOOR OPENING

HEIGHT:	MAX. 2,254 m 7'4 3/4"
	MIN. 1,997 m 6'6 5/8"
WIDTH:	MAX. 2,350 m 7'8 1/2"
	MIN. 2,118 m 6'11 3/8"

TARE WEIGHT (UNLADEN WEIGHT)

MAX. 4,350 kg 9,590 pounds
MIN. 3,790 kg 8,750 pounds

OUTSIDE DIMENSIONS

LENGTH:	12,190 m 40'0"
HEIGHT:	MAX. 2,590 m 8'6"
	MIN. 2.438 m 8'0"
WIDTH:	2,438 m 8'0"

40 FT. REEFER CONTAINERS

INSIDE DIMENSIONS

LENGTH:	MAX. 11,210 m 36'9 9/16"
	MIN. 11,124 m 36'6"
HEIGHT:	MAX. 2,240 m 7'4 5/16"
	MIN. 2,184 m 7'2"
WIDTH:	MAX. 2,238 m 7'4 1/18"
	MIN. 2,159 m 7'1"

INTERNAL CUBIC CAPACITY

MAX. 57,0 CBM 2006 cubic feet
MIN. 54,4 CBM 1930 cubic feet

MAX GROSS CAPACITY

MAX. 24,730 kg 54,550 pounds
MIN 24,566 kg 54,160 pounds

DOOR OPENING

HEIGHT:	MAX. 2,190 m 7'2 3/16"
	MIN. 2,057 m 6'9"
WIDTH:	MAX. 2,238 m 7'4 1/8"
	MIN. 2,172 m 7' 1/8"

TARE WEIGHT (UNLADEN WEIGHT)

MAX. 5,915 kg 13,040 pounds
MIN. 5,740 kg 12,660 pounds

OUTSIDE DIMENSIONS

LENGTH:	12,190 m 40'0"
HEIGHT:	2,590 m 8'6"
WIDTH:	2,438 m 8'0"

20 FOOT CONTAINER 8 x 8 x 20' Main deck container

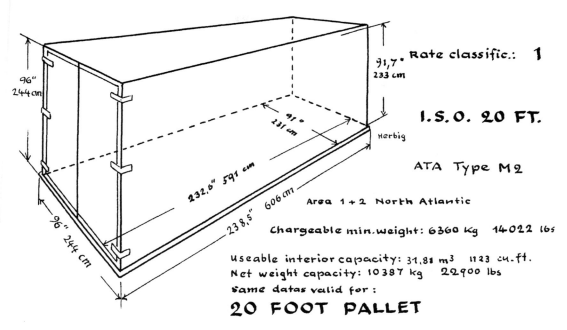

Rate classific.: 1

I.S.O. 20 FT.

ATA Type M2

Area 1+2 North Atlantic

Chargeable min. weight: 6360 kg   14022 lbs

Useable interior capacity: 31,81 m³   1123 cu.ft.
Net weight capacity: 10387 kg   22900 lbs
same datas valid for:

20 FOOT PALLET

10 FOOT CONTAINER 8 x 8 x 10' Main deck container

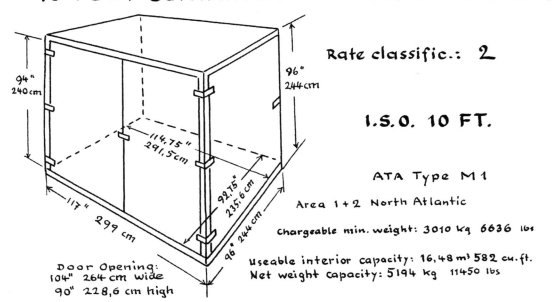

Rate classific.: 2

I.S.O. 10 FT.

ATA Type M1

Area 1+2 North Atlantic

Chargeable min. weight: 3010 kg 6636 lbs

Useable interior capacity: 16,48 m³ 582 cu.ft.
Net weight capacity: 5194 kg 11450 lbs

Door Opening:
104" 264 cm wide
90" 228,6 cm high

FULL 125" PALLET w. NET

for high capacity aircraft

96"
244 cm

Rate classific.: **2a**

85" 216 cm

122" 310 cm

88" 224 cm

318 cm

125"

ATA Type M1

Area 1 + 2 North Atlantic

Chargeable min. weight: 2820 kg 6217 lbs

Useable cube capacity: 16,3 m³ 575 cu.ft.
Net weight capacity: 5892,4 kg 12990 lbs

Rate classific.: **2aa** **125" IGLOO** for high capacity aircraft

88" x 125" x 88" 224 cm x 318 cm x 224 cm
Useable cube capacity: 14,80 m³ 523 cu.ft.
chargeable min. weight: 2615 kg 5765 lbs

FULL 125" PALLET w. NET

for high capacity aircraft

72"
183 cm

Rate classific.: **2b**

93" 236 cm

122" 310 cm

96" 244 cm

125" 318 cm

Area 1 + 2 North Atlantic

Chargeable min. weight: 2315 kg 5104 lbs

Useable cube capacity: 13,3 m³ 470 cu.ft.
Net weight capacity: 6800 kg 15000 lbs

FULL 125" PALLET WITH NET

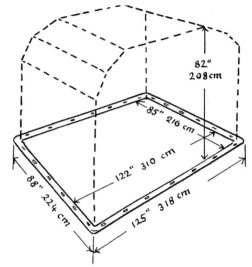

82"
208cm

85" 216 cm

122" 310 cm

88" 224 cm

125" 318 cm

Rate classific.: **3**

Area 1 + 2 North Atlantic

Chargeable min.wgt: 2100 kg   4630 lbs

Useable cube capacity: 12,97 m³ 458 cu.ft.
Net wgt. capacity: 5892,4 kg 12990 lbs

ATA Types A1   A2   A3

FULL 125" JGLOO

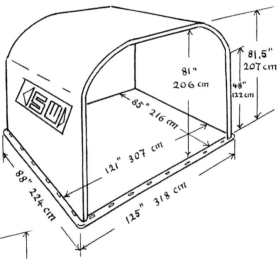

81,5"
207cm

81"
206 cm

48"
122cm

85" 216 cm

121" 307 cm

88" 224 cm

125" 318 cm

Rate classific.: **3**

Area 1 + 2 North Atlantic

chargeable min.wgt: 2100 kg   4630 lbs

Useable inerior cap.: 12,6 m³   445 cu.ft.
Net weight capacity: 5783.5 kg 12750 lbs

ATA Types A1   A2 A3

FULL 125" JGLOO - QC

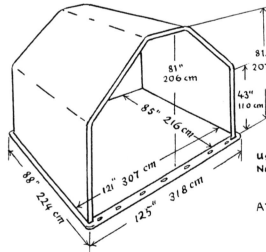

81.5"
207cm

81"
206cm

43"
110 cm

85" 216 cm

121" 307 cm

88" 224 cm

125" 318 cm

Rate classific.: **3**

Area 1 + 2 North Atlantic

Chargeable min.wgt: 2100 kg 4630 lbs

Useable interior cap.: 11,7 m³ 413 cu.ft.
Net weight capacity: 5797 kg 12780 lbs

ATA Types: A1   A2   A3

LOWER DECK STRUCTURAL JGLOO 125"

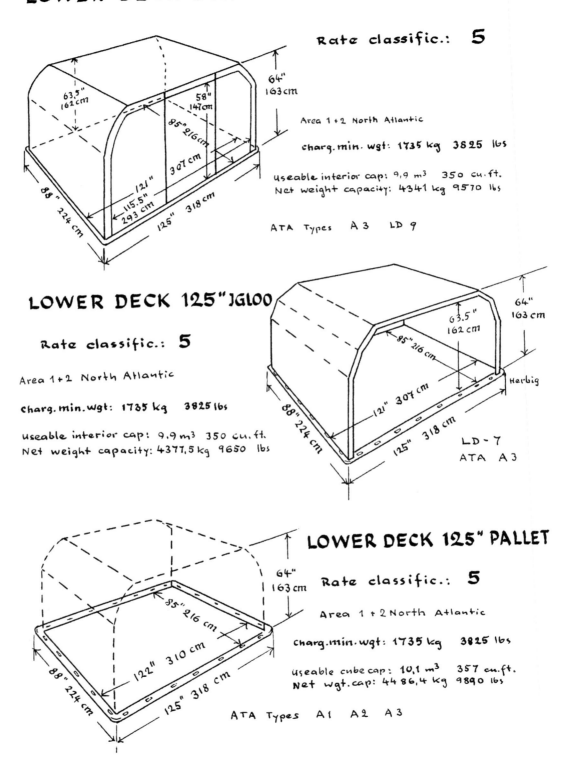

Rate classific.: 5

63,5" 162cm

58" 147cm

64" 163cm

85" 216 cm

307 cm

121"

115.5" 293 cm

88" 224 cm

125" 318 cm

Area 1+2 North Atlantic

charg. min. wgt: 1735 kg   3825 lbs

useable interior cap: 9,9 m³   350 cu.ft.
Net weight capacity: 4341 kg 9570 lbs

ATA Types   A 3   LD 9

LOWER DECK 125" JGLOO

Rate classific.: 5

Area 1+2 North Atlantic

charg. min. wgt: 1735 kg   3825 lbs

useable interior cap: 9,9 m³ 350 cu.ft.
Net weight capacity: 4377,5 kg 9650 lbs

63.5" 162 cm

64" 163 cm

85" 216 cm

121" 307 cm

Herbig

88" 224 cm

125" 318 cm

LD - 7
ATA A 3

LOWER DECK 125" PALLET

Rate classific.: 5

Area 1 + 2 North Atlantic

charg. min. wgt: 1735 kg   3825 lbs

useable cube cap: 10,1 m³   357 cu.ft.
Net wgt. cap: 4486,4 kg 9890 lbs

ATA Types   A1   A2   A3

64" 163cm

85" 216 cm

122" 310 cm

88" 224 cm

125" 318 cm

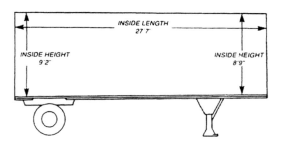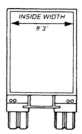

15 Series–2,061 Cubic Feet

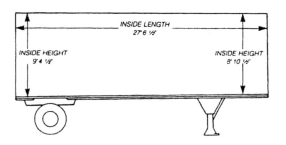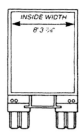

17–19 Series Double Trailer–2,100 Cubic Feet

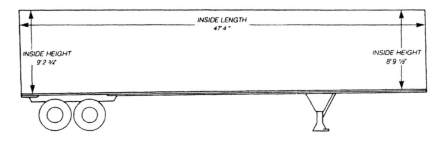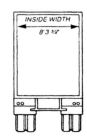

79 Series Semi Trailer–3,560 Cubic Feet

Appendix G

This section includes some helpful packaging tips.

■ **DON'T** nail or staple into the end grain. This reduces the strength of the crate by up to 35 percent.

END GRAIN

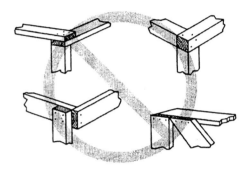

SIDE GRAIN

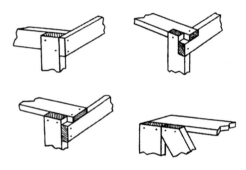

■ **DON'T** use gummed labels on wood as they do not adhere very well and are often lost to abrasion.

A crate's strength should be matched to the weight and density of the product to be shipped. Crate strengths ensure product safety throughout the transportation process.

RELATIVE STRENGTH

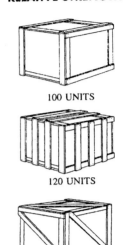

100 UNITS

120 UNITS

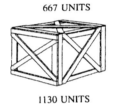

667 UNITS

1130 UNITS

PROPER STACKING

■ Cartons should be stacked squarely on the pallet, one precisely on top of the other. This takes the weight off of the product inside the carton.

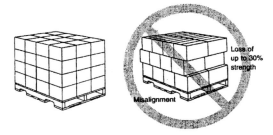

■ Interlocking stacking patterns result in the loss of up to 50 percent of the cartons' top-to-bottom compression strength.

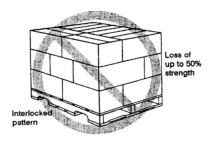

■ Align cartons flush with pallet. Misaligned and overhanging cartons result in loss of compression strength of up to 32 percent.

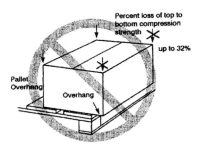

■ Create a level surface for maximum strength and stability. Pyramid pallet loads do not provide a level surface and top cartons are exposed to potential damage and loss. Single cartons should be shipped loose to prevent damage.

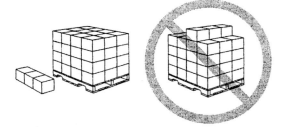

■ Properly stacked cartons should be secured in place by banding, breakaway adhesive or shrink wrap (as detailed on previous page).

■ Properly stacked cartons provide greater stability when being moved with a pallet jack or forklift.

CRATING

Crating your shipments can help ensure safe and damage-free transit if it is done properly and good quality lumber is used. Here are a few "do's" and "don'ts" when constructing shipping crates:

■ DO fasten (immobilize) crated contents to the base.

■ DO fully enclose the product. Accurately show how the product should be loaded with arrows and other directional indications.

■ DO provide adequate flooring to prevent damage by forklift blades.

Glossary

Accessorial Charges: Extra charges assessed by a carrier for a special service performed by the carrier for the shipper or consignee.

Automatic Identification: A collection of interrelated technologies that allow for automated collection of data. The most common types of Auto ID technologies are bar codes and radio-frequency identification.

Bill of Lading: A shipping document that serves as a contract of carriage, a receipt from the carrier to the shipper for the goods tendered and a presumption of title to the goods.

Bit: The smallest single unit of data that can be represented within a computer.

Broker: A company that matches the freight of a shipper with an owner-operator. Brokers typically do not own their own trucks. They perform all of the administrative functions of dispatching and freight invoicing.

Bureau of Export Administration (BXA): A U.S. government agency responsible for developing the regulations governing exports from the United States.

Business Logistics: The business discipline that typically encompasses the functional areas of transportation, purchasing, inventory management, warehousing and import/export operations.

Byte: A collection of 8 bits.

Central Processing Unit (CPU): The location within a computer where the actual computing takes place.

Class Rate System: A system of grouping freight with similar transportation characteristics that was developed to simplify the rating of freight.

Collect: The consignee pays the freight charges for a freight movement.

Commodity Rate: A freight rate developed for a specific commodity for movement between two specified points.

Computer Program: A detailed set of instructions telling the computer to perform a specific task.

Consignee: The person receiving the freight.

Consignor: The person shipping the freight.

Customs Broker: An intermediary organization that acts as an importer's agent with U.S. Customs. Customs brokers calculate the appropriate customs duty owed on import shipments and process the necessary paperwork to allow for the release of imported goods from Customs' custody.

Detention/Demurrage: An extra charge assessed by a carrier for an excessive amount of waiting time.

Dimensional Weight: The practice of an air carrier charging more for bulky freight than for dense freight. This is also known as dimensionalizing or dimming.

Duty: A tax collected by a government on imported goods.

Electronic Data Interchange (EDI): A means of electronically transmitting business data from one company's computer system to that of a another company.

Economic Order Quantity The lowest annual total cost occurs at the order quantity where inventory carrying costs equal acquisition costs.

Filed Rate Doctrine:	A provision of the Interstate Commerce Act requiring a carrier to file their rates with the ICC. This is no longer in effect.
Free on Board (FOB):	This references various terms of sales. The FOB point indicates where the title to the goods passes and who has responsibility for the freight charges.
Freight Forwarder:	An intermediary that consolidates the freight of many shippers into a larger shipment that is then tendered to a carrier for shipment.
Freight-All-Kinds (FAK) Rate:	A mutual agreement between a shipper and a carrier allowing goods of different freight classes to be rated under one class rating. This is a means of simplifying the rating process for a shipper of multiple products.
Harmonized System:	A uniform commodity classification system to simplify the assessment of duty on imported products.
Incoterms:	International Commercial Terms. International terms of sale. These are very similar in purpose to FOB terms.
Integrated Carriers:	An organization that owns its own aircraft and forwards freight to commercial airlines. They provide pick-up and delivery service with their own equipment as well. They are also known as integrators.
Interlining:	The practice of having more than one carrier complete a transportation movement.
Inter-Modal:	The practice of moving freight stowed in truck trailers or ocean containers via rail. This is also known as piggyback service, trailer-on-flat-car (TOFC) or container-on-flat-car (COFC).
Internet:	A computer network originally developed by the U.S. Department of Defense that was designed to be indestructible, even in the event of a nuclear attack. Now a global communications network.

Interstate Commerce Commission (ICC): A government agency established by the Act to Regulate Commerce of 1887. Its purpose was to curb abuses within the U.S. transportation industry. It is now defunct.

Just-In-Time (JIT): The practice that requires the consumption of resources at the last possible moment relative to production for customer demand.

Less-Than-Truckload (LTL): A shipment that does not fill the capacity of a truck trailer.

Letter of Credit (L/C): A negotiable instrument used in conducting international sales transactions.

Local Area Network (LAN): A method of connecting personal computers and various computing equipment within the confines of the same general geographic area.

Logistics: A military term referring to the movement of troops, equipment and supplies from one location to another.

Long-Haul Carrier: A carrier serving destinations greater than 300 miles from its origin.

National Motor Freight Classification (NMFC): The trucking industry's governing class rating guide.

Non-Vessel Operating Common Carrier (NVOCC): A non-asset based ocean freight provider.

North American Free Trade Agreement: A treaty between the United States, Canada and Mexico that allows for duty-free or reduced duty treatment of goods produced in any of these countries.

Pareto's Law: 20% of your assignments account for 80% of your time. Also known as the 80-20 rule.

Point-to-Point Rate: A flat price for a specified volume of freight between two named points. These are usually determined by the mileage between the two points.

Prepaid: The shipper pays the freight charges for a freight movement.

Prepay and Add: The shipper pays the carrier for a freight move, but then invoices the consignee for these same charges.

Random Access Memory (RAM): The memory space in which users run their computer programs. Anything stored in RAM is lost when the power to the computer is turned-off.

Rate Bureaus: Organizations that develop rates for groups of carriers.

Read-Only Memory (ROM): Non-volatile memory that contains basic instruction to the computer. Under normal circumstances, it cannot be altered by the user.

Reconsignment: Changing the destination for a shipment already in-transit.

Reefer: A refrigerated trailer or ocean container.

Schedule B: The governing tariff for classifying exports from the United States.

Short-Haul Carrier: A carrier serving destinations less than 300 miles from its origin.

Surface Transportation Board (Surf Board): An agency within the Department of Transportation that has taken over the remaining responsibilities of the former ICC.

Tariff: A schedule of rates or rules.

Third-Party Billing: Someone other than the shipper or the consignee pays the carrier charges for a freight move.

Truckload (TL): A shipment of such size that it fills-out the visible capacity of a truck trailer or that weighs in excess of 36,000 pounds.

Uniform Freight Classification (UFC): The rail industry's governing class rating guide.

UNIX: A multi-user, multi-tasking computer operating system.

World Wide Web (WWW): The graphical interface placed on top of the Internet. The Internet is the network; the Web is the stuff on the network.

Index

About the Author

Mike Stroh has been a logistics practitioner since 1979. He has served in a variety of operational and administrative positions in a diverse range of industries including wearing apparel, footwear, automotive, machinery, metals and hazardous chemicals. His titles have included transportation manager and purchasing manager.

He is a graduate of the Academy of Advanced Traffic. He has a BS in Transportation from St. John's University, New York and a MBA in Global Management from the University of Phoenix. Finally, he is a member of the Council of Logistics Management (CLM), a certified member of the American Society of Transportation & Logistics (AST&L) and the International Society of Logistics (SOLE).

Currently, he operates *logisticsnetwork.com*, an Internet-based logistics service provider. *logisticnetwork.com* provides to the logistics community a vehicle for conducting logistics research, a connection to major logistics providers and support organizations, a logistics forum to discuss relevant issues facing the logistics community, a free answerback service and a very vibrant employment clearinghouse. In addition, he teaches international trade and transportation at the School of International Trade and Commerce of Pace University, New York, NY.